DON'T
FORGET
THE
ACCENT
MARK

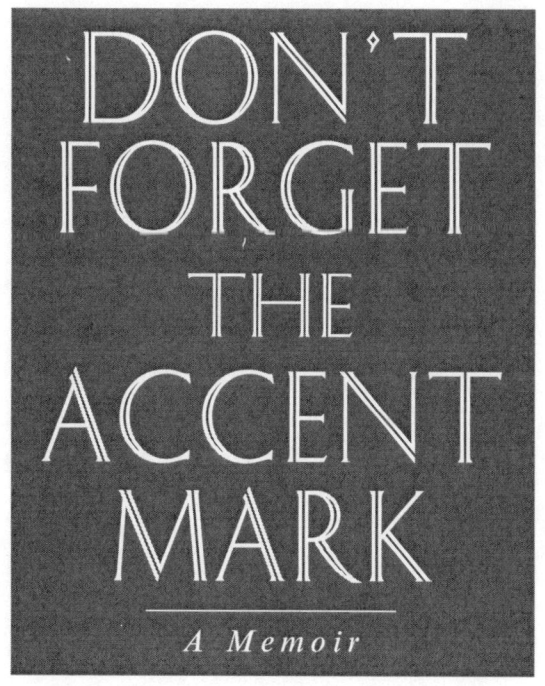

DON'T FORGET THE ACCENT MARK

A Memoir

David A. Sánchez

University of New Mexico Press

Albuquerque

Library of Congress Cataloging-in-Publication Data

Sánchez, David A.
Don't forget the accent mark : a memoir / David A. Sánchez.
   p. cm.
ISBN 978-0-8263-5047-3 (pbk. : alk. paper)
1. Sánchez, David A.
2. Hispanic Americans—Biography.
I. Title.

E184.S75S25 2011
978.9'053092—dc22
[B]

                    2010050450

CONTENTS

PROLOGUE

These writings could be regarded as the success story of a young man raised in a family of modest income, who was gifted in mathematics, went to college, served as a Marine Corps officer, received a doctorate, taught at excellent universities, and worked as a senior university and federal administrator. This is commendable but nothing really worth writing about; there are not just a few who have followed the same paths. But the important facts are that the young man was of mixed parentage (Mexican and American), was raised in a Mexican home in an Anglo, middle-class, California neighborhood, and was fluent in Spanish and English when he entered kindergarten.

His last name was garden-variety Spanish, but he was fair skinned; his English was unaccented; and his Spanish was pure Mexican. None of this should have had any influence on the career path he chose, but at certain moments it did. With the birth of the Chicano Movement and affirmative action, a different and sometimes disturbing significance became attached to his name. This story chronicles his life and those moments.

CHAPTER ONE

EARLY DAYS

Sanchez is a pretty common name in the southwestern United States. More properly it should be spelled Sánchez, as I was informed by my grandfather Cecilio shortly after I moved into my Mexican grandparents' home in San Diego, California, at the age of three. I asked him what was the funny mark above our name, and he sternly replied, "*Asi se escribe nuestro nombre en esta familia*" (In this family that is the way our name is written). Don Cecilio was not a person to be disobeyed, so whenever I sign my name, the accent mark is always there—a little symbol of my Mexicanness in the Anglo world in which I was raised.

Growing up, the accent was not a problem, except for a few raised eyebrows now and then because I look more Irish or Welsh than Mexican. But when I was in training in the Marine Corps, we were required to stencil our names on our utility shirts. I decided to add the accent mark, which really angered one of my drill instructors. He asked me what it was, and I replied as my grandfather had done. He loudly accused me of being some kind of a French pervert or a communist sympathizer; uniformity is a very strict requirement of Marine Corps training, even on stencils. I stood rigidly at the best USMC attention, just as loudly repeated my reason, and after a few more insults, the DI stormed off. I never heard any more about it.

Nowadays you see the name Sanchez everywhere. There are writers, artists, entertainers, military personnel at all levels, news commentators, athletes, politicians, and scholars, many of them with the first name David. But well into my early middle age, I rarely encountered a namesake, and I regarded myself as a typical American but with the advantage of being bilingual. No English was spoken in my grandparents' house. When I arrived, I only spoke English, but my grandfather insisted that every Sunday we have a Spanish lesson, using some of the old primers he used as a boy in Mexico in the late eighteen hundreds. When I entered kindergarten, I could already read and speak Spanish. Since there were only two Mexican families in our neighborhood, Mission Hills (middle to upper class then, but now much more posh), it was English out the door and Spanish in the door.

In the thirties and early forties, San Diego had a population of about two hundred thousand, with a sizeable Mexican population largely living in the Logan Heights neighborhood. We would visit friends there frequently; many of them were families whose parents had fled Mexico during the Mexican Revolution, just as my grandparents had done. Birthday and holiday fiestas, lively events in which I enthusiastically participated, were packed with our Mexican friends, which certainly enhanced my appreciation and acceptance of my heritage.

Statistics on the composition of today's Latino households shows many families in which the grandparents are raising the children, usually for reasons such as an illegitimate birth or a broken marriage. Many of these grandparents are trying to protect the family structure and reputation and want to insure that the child is raised in a loving environment with attention being paid to its education. The Mexican grandparental culture is a strong, supportive one from which I certainly benefited.

How did I acquire the name Sánchez? I was born in 1933 in San Francisco, probably out of wedlock, the son of Berta Sánchez and a man I prefer not to identify. (I did not know his name until I was seventeen, when my grandmother had to emotionally provide my birth certificate in order for me to apply to the Navy Reserve.) When I was three years old, my mother decided to move back to Mexico; she was bilingual and a skilled secretary, so there were good job opportunities. But she had no confidence in the Mexican medical system and did not wish the stigma of being an unwed mother. So she arranged for me to be raised in San Diego by my grand-parents, Cecilio and Concepcion Sánchez.

Probably for reasons of legitimacy and propriety, my grandparents decided to adopt me, and I became a member of the Sánchez clan—my grandparents, two uncles, and an aunt, all living in San Diego; my mother, at least ten Mexican great-uncles and -aunts, plus many cousins. Legally, I was my own uncle! I called my grandparents Padre Cecilio and Madre Cons, but it did not take long to figure out that they were not my parents. That was not a real emotional problem, since they and my uncles lovingly raised me.

My mother remarried in Mexico but returned frequently to visit and to give birth to her two children in a San Diego hospital. My grandparents referred to her as my aunt Berta, but she treated me in such a way that I concluded that she was my mother. When I was eleven years old, I confronted her with my conclusion. She confessed but made me promise that it was our little secret and not to let the rest of the family know of my discovery. No problem.

Over the years my half siblings, Juan Marcelo Duarte, who lives in Idaho, and Berta Micaela (Miki) Duarte, who lives near Mexico City, and I have been very close, and despite my mother's wishes, I felt obligated to let them know our relationship. When they were teenagers, I disclosed my status and swore them to secrecy. At Aunt Berta's eightieth birthday party in Mexico City, she revealed the truth to assembled friends and relatives. I'm sure many of them had long suspected it.

The identity of my father was more troubling. When I found out his full name, I would look it up in telephone directories whenever I traveled around the country while in college and the service. Finally, when I was twenty-six, married with a family and finishing my tour of duty in the Marine Corps, I cornered my uncle Marcelo and insisted that I was entitled to whatever information about my father he had. I was stunned when he told me that my father was the manager of a fashionable, downtown men's and boys' clothing store where my grandmother would take me to shop once or twice a year when I was a youngster. So I went to the store and introduced myself to my father. We exchanged a few pleasantries, I took one last look, then said good-bye. I have never contacted him again. I always marvel at Madre Cons's wisdom in arranging those encounters without compromising her values and my father's privacy.

Padre Cecilio was a dapper dresser, spoke little English, and commuted by bus every day to Tijuana, where he was the chief accountant of a major Baja California liquor distributor. Madre Cons had a beautiful complexion, spoke accented but good English, and was a loyal member of the Sociedad de Santa Rita, a Catholic charitable organization. She had pictures of the Virgin Mary and Franklin Roosevelt side by side in her prayer niche. "We wouldn't have this house without their help," she told me.

At one of the meetings of the Sociedad, the archbishop attended. When Madre Cons told me to get in line and kiss his ring, I loudly protested, *"Madre Cons, tiene microbios!"* A silence fell over the assembled Mexican ladies; it was broken when the prelate gave a hearty laugh.

During the Mexican Revolution (1910–1917), Padre Cecilio was a Mexican government employee, which meant that some days he had a desk and other days he had to run for his life. Two itinerant Methodist missionaries suggested to him that they could take his two boys, my uncles Sergio and Marcelo, to the Spanish-American Institute in Gardena, California, where they would be safe, learn English, and be provided a vocational education. He agreed and also sent Madre Cons and the two girls to Tijuana. He then fled from the interior of Mexico to El Paso and then hitchhiked to Tijuana. Later, the family reunited in San Diego, where they bought a home and the children completed their education at San Diego High School.

Padre Cecilio repaid the Methodist Church by enrolling me in Sunday School at the Mission Hills Methodist Church instead of my going to catechism at nearby St. Vincent de Paul church. This was very hurtful to my grandmother, who told me there was a black mark in her celestial report card because I was not raised a Catholic. She would exclaim, "Gracias a Dios!" whenever I told her I was dating a Catholic girl. But I was baptized Catholic, would accompany Madre Cons to religious ceremonies at the Mexican Catholic church in Logan Heights, and would go light candles for her when she was ill. Entering a classic Catholic church, especially in Mexico, with the statues of the saints, the gilded altar, flickering candles, and sometimes skeletons, and comparing it to the austere Protestant sanctuaries I had seen, always convinced me that God lived in Catholic churches.

Skin color always fascinated me. Madre Cons and Aunt Berta were fair complected, Padre Cecilio less so, Uncles Sergio and Marcelo were swarthy Mexican males, Aunt Estela was a brown Latin bombshell, and half sister Miki's skin was so pale she could pass for a Dresden doll. When I visited

Mexico, I saw all shades of skin colors, but the lovely ladies in the TV advertisements looked just like the ones on the U.S. screen, except there were fewer blondes. I discovered that in certain segments of the Mexican society, there was a prejudice against darker skin; the description *"es muy India"* was not a flattering one.

I attended Grant Grammar School from kindergarten to the sixth grade starting in September 1937; there were no Mexican or black students in the school. The seven years were pretty uneventful, but I did acquire the trait of talking a lot in class and being a cutup. My report cards showed a string of As and Bs on the scholarship side all through to high school and mostly Ds and Fs on the deportment side—getting a C was cause for celebration.

My Mexicanness was very personal: it was my home life and was shared with my family and their friends. I had this special gift of bilingualism, but otherwise considered myself to be an average American kid. I remember that my third- or fourth-grade teacher convinced my grandmother to dress me up in a charro outfit and have me sing the Mexican national anthem ("Mexicanos, al grito de guerra") at an outdoor all-school assembly. I felt like an exotic insect on display in front of my Anglo classmates. I ran home afterward and cried a lot.

I played a lot of playground basketball, a sport I pursued until my forties, but spent a lot of time in my beloved room with my books and magic tricks. My grandfather gave me my first two books in English, which I still have—a history of science and the collected stories of Sherlock Holmes. When I was nine years old, Madre Cons presented me with a junior-size rod and reel and some hooks and sinkers. She packed a lunch, and we took the bus to the Mission Bay Bridge, where she sat on a lawn chair with an umbrella while I fished all day. There were no fishermen in our family, so I don't know where she got the idea, but the disease stuck—I have fished nearly two hundred waters in this country and abroad.

The only major event I can remember from those days was one Sunday afternoon when Padre Cecilio and I rode the bus downtown to the San Diego High School stadium to watch a semipro football team, the San Diego Bombers, play. Around halftime, it was announced over the PA system that the game would be stopped and we were to go home as quickly as possible. It was December 7, 1941, and the Japanese had bombed Pearl Harbor. I remember the hush that fell over the stadium.

My grandfather was a taciturn man; I never heard him speak a word of English, but I suspected he knew it very well. He would arise, eat breakfast, administer his insulin injection in his thigh, which I always marveled at, then get dressed and leave for his seventeen-mile bus commute to Tijuana. He would return in early evening, eat dinner, then read until bedtime, his pack of Lucky Strikes at hand—he was not to be disturbed. On Sundays, after I came home from Sunday School, he would give me my Spanish lesson, for which I received fifteen cents. In the afternoon, we all might go to Balboa Park for an outdoor organ concert or to the San Diego Zoo. I have never lost my love of zoos, especially the reptile houses; this probably came from reading the adventures of African big game hunters, explorers, and animal collectors.

At parties and family gatherings, Padre Cecilio was a much livelier person. He would challenge guests to create long columns of figures to add and race for the answer, which he would usually have before they wrote down their first digit. He was also acknowledged as a master dry-martini mixer. These talents were inherited by my uncle Sergio, who used his calculational skills as a bookmaker until he was arrested. Later he became a very skilled professional bartender. My other uncle, Marcelo, followed the commercial line and was an assistant branch manager for Bank of America. None of my family went to college, though I suspect my grandfather went beyond secondary school in Mexico.

Both uncles were excellent foster fathers. Their celebrations and parties were a great help in my developing an acceptance of people from diverse walks of life, whom I would not encounter in Mission Hills or later in my academic life. At these events I met business people, construction workers, tuna fishermen, gamblers, and maybe some shady characters. They were Anglos, Mexicans, Greeks, and Italians. This helped me a lot as I worked my way through school employed in grocery stores, shipyards, and military surplus stores. When I would come home from graduate school, where I studied mathematics, I was always warmly received, but often quizzically asked "Are you still in school?"

My uncle Marcelo was the serious one. He appointed himself as my moral and financial advisor, but his lectures were short and infrequent, unless he got on the topic of liberals. He would line up fishing dates for me with some of his associates who had boats. My uncle Sergio was the gregarious and sports loving one, who would take me to baseball games, the horse races at Del Mar, and prizefights at the San Diego Coliseum. He was a Navy boxing instructor during World War II and was a well-known figure in the San Diego fight scene, frequently in the corner of local professionals. He once had an automobile accident and injured his knee, so he recuperated at our house; I prided myself on having the only bathroom in Mission Hills with copies of *The Ring* magazine.

The summer after my fifth grade, I visited my mother (still Aunt Berta), her two children (my half brother, Juan, and my half sister, Miki), and her husband, Juan, from whom she later separated. He was a member of the Mexican Consular Corps and was working in the border town of Nogales, Arizona, where the family had a spacious apartment. I loved the desert environs and always looked forward to encountering a dangerous insect or reptile. I was mesmerized by the exotic family maid, a Yaqui Indian woman, who would invite me to her room, sit me on the floor, then sit across from me with her can of tobacco and papers in her lap, sing strange songs and roll cigarettes.

My grandmother was an outgoing person who was able to communicate very well in her accented English. The clerks and managers of the local Safeway and Piggly Wiggly stores would always greet her warmly, and the pharmacist-owner of the Ace Drugstore would patiently listen to her discussions of her various ailments. The drugstore had an old-fashioned soda fountain with a marble counter and pedestal seats, and on Saturdays I was allowed to order my favorite—a grilled cheese sandwich and chocolate malt—and put it on the charge account. The shops of Mission Hills served most of our needs, but at least once a month Madre Cons and I would ride the bus downtown to shop at the big department stores, Walkers and Marstons. If I got to visit the toy sections, this was okay, but sometimes she would greatly embarrass me by making me carry her flowery umbrella or sit in the ladies' lingerie section while she shopped for underwear.

Aside from family parties there was very little social interaction in our Mission Hills home. We did get along fine with our two neighbor families, who would often watch me after school if grandmother was not home. But almost all of our celebrations took place at fiestas at family homes in Logan Heights, the Mexican district. Many of those families were immigrants who had fled Mexico during the revolution, just like my grandparents. Most of the older men had jobs as clerks or salesmen in Spanish-speaking businesses; one owned a shoe-repair shop. They would sometimes have lengthy conversations with me about my future, encouraging me to take lots of mathematics and science courses, and occasionally discussing some scientific theories. I always wondered where this understanding came from, and it was much later in my life that I realized these were all highly skilled men who had had to flee Mexico during the Revolution and take up less prestigious jobs—the shoe-repair shop owner was an electrical engineer. I'm sure that in the thirties and forties there were pockets of individuals like them all across the Mexican border.

I could see that it was difficult for my grandparents to advise and instruct me. They had raised their children in old Mexico and were now confronted with a California teenager in the booming forties and fifties. Their moral standards were high, and they did a good job, but once in awhile they would insist on my observing Mexican tradition. For instance, my grandmother was strongly opposed to the notion of Dutch treat, having once been invited by some American ladies to lunch, then asked to pay her share of the bill. She was shocked. In Mexico and most Latin countries, if you invite, you pay, unless you are family or very close friends. I would often be lectured about this reprehensible American custom before going on a date; Madre Cons never knew how many times allowance money would be pooled to pay for the movie tickets.

A major figure in my early guidance was my Sunday School teacher, Dr. Maurice Brown, an eminent surgeon and a very Christian man. He started off with a small group of fifth-grade boys and was our teacher through high school. He would often have class at early dawn at Mission Bay, where we would cook breakfast, have Bible study, and then go for a ride in his motorboat. He was a wonderful model for me of what it was like to lead a Christian life, and in later years, when Madre Cons's health deteriorated, he would stop by the house and advise her. I took care of his garden when he and his family would go on vacation. This along with other odd jobs and babysitting were my sources of income. I never learned to ride a bicycle, so I couldn't qualify for a newspaper delivery route.

I can say my early days through grammar school were normal but had additional connections to Mexico through my home, language, family, and friends. I never thought much about my name or how I had acquired it until later in life; for me it was no different than all the other names in my school—Anglo-Saxon, German, Italian. My classmates might have been a little bothered when they came into my house to play and I only spoke Spanish to my grandmother, but they got used to it pretty quickly. In my thinking, I was just an American kid who happened to also speak excellent Spanish and have Mexican parents.

CHAPTER TWO

SECONDARY
SCHOOL DAYS

In the fall of 1944, most of my Mission Hills sixth-grade class was enrolled in the seventh grade at Horace Mann Junior High School, located at the intersection of Park and El Cajon Boulevards, about two miles away and requiring two transfers on the city buses. The school building, torn down long ago, was a magnificent but fading domed structure with beautiful porticos and graceful columns; it had been a school administrative building previously. We were joined by students, all white and middle class, from the Hillcrest and University Heights districts. One Mexican student from El Paso transferred into the eighth grade, but only stayed one year. He never wanted to speak Spanish with me, possibly because he was never allowed to speak it in school in Texas.

In junior high school I developed a dramatic flair and starred in several one-act plays and some slapstick skits for school assemblies. I continued disrupting classes, and one of my highlights occurred one day when our fuddy-duddy mathematics teacher, who spent much of the class time telling us stories about his travels in China, left the room. The classroom was on the second floor, so I tied his chair to the venetian blinds cord and tossed it out the window. I did get kicked out of school for one day for uttering a mildly profane greeting to one of my buddies in the hallway.

One summer, Madre Cons decided that she and I were going to take the Southern Pacific train from San Diego to Mexico City to visit Aunt Berta, her two children, and seemingly countless female relatives in Mexico City, Guadalajara, and Guanajuato, many of whom were very affectionate. I fell in love with at least three cousins who were four or five years older than me. The thrill of the trip was visiting a family home in Penjamo. It was said that treasure was buried in the courtyard to keep Pancho Villa's revolutionary troops from taking it. An additional exciting feature was that there was a ghost who would appear at midnight carrying a lantern, looking for the treasure. It must have been his night off when I stayed up until the early hours to see him.

I loved Mexico, especially the museums and the huge city mercados, where I could wander for hours talking to the vendors, looking at the exotic meats and fruits, and buying some knickknacks. Later in life, when I was a professor of mathematics, I frequently was invited to Mexico City to give lectures or teach a course; I discovered that while I could lecture in Spanish, I could not explain the mathematical symbols in Spanish as I wrote them on the blackboard without becoming almost totally tongue-tied. I had learned my arithmetic and mathematics in English; translating an equation immediately into Spanish was very difficult and completely destroyed the presentation. So I would apologize to my audience, rattle off my symbols in English—*equis* was "x," *mas* was "+"—then turn around and comfortably explain the significance of the equations in Spanish. The audience found this amusing.

In the ninth grade my algebra teacher informed me that I had scored the top grade in a citywide mathematics test. This had little impact, since I couldn't see how it would help

my planned future career as a mentalist/magician/escape art-
ist. At that time I was doing magic shows for church dinners
and birthday parties to earn a few dollars, and I was a junior
member of the city magic club. A highlight was when the great
illusionist, John Calvert, brought his spectacular show to the
Orpheum Theater, and the club members were given front-
row seats and got to meet Calvert afterward. I did a few mentalism acts at fraternity parties while in college, and to this day
the wife of one of my classmates swears that I read her mind.

Mentalism, or mind reading as it is popularly called, was
my favorite form of magic. I revered the books of the famous
nightclub mentalist Ted Anneman, and ordered by mail some
of his effects from magic shops in Los Angeles and New York.
What I liked about mentalism was that it didn't require all the
gimmicky apparatus that magicians use, and relied mostly
on slips of paper, playing cards, chalk and slates, and maybe
a telephone directory. The problem is that as an eleven- or
twelve-year-old, you can't convince an audience of your supposed powers of mental transference and telepathy—"reading
minds." So I was stuck with doing parlor tricks. It made more
sense when I was older and in college, but by then studies and
interest in girls got in the way, so I had to put mentalism and
magic aside.

As our ninth-grade year was ending, the class realized that
most of us would be joining our rival, Roosevelt Junior High,
another all-white student body, and moving on to San Diego
High School, the central city high school, with two thousand–
plus students. We were apprehensive because about a quarter
of those students came from the Logan Heights district, which
had a high percentage of black and Mexican families. There
were tales of gangs, getting beat up, and being "pantsed"—
having your pants pulled down in the hallways. But by the
first month our fears were allayed. Social groups were being

formed around sports and clubs, and the school was well on the way to becoming a model American high school.

The high school was often referred to as the "Gray Castle," because it was comprised of several majestic, ivy covered, two-story stone classroom buildings connected with graceful walkways and fronted by a beautiful lawn and landscaping. In the twenties it was used to represent a college in some Hollywood films. Eventually it was too expensive to maintain and in the seventies was torn down and replaced by some version of the standard, ugly, American school building. However, the massive wooden doors that formed the entrance to the main building were preserved—incongruous but magnificent reminders of the past.

The most wonderful three years of my life were my time at San Diego High School, a model central city high school drawing from every ethnic neighborhood. There were Anglos, largely from two large junior high schools, Mexicans and blacks from Logan Heights and Memorial Junior High, Greeks and Italians, many of whose families were the backbone of the tuna-fishing industry, and a fair size population of Filipino, Nisei, and Chinese students. My name and I fit right in. The 1950 population of San Diego was about 335,000; it was just recovering from World War II, and the enthusiasm and optimism were reflected in the spirit of the high school. I have attended nearly every class reunion, the last being my sixtieth, and in 1995, I was elected to the San Diego High School Wall of Honor.

In San Diego in the late forties and the fifties, the issues of racism and discrimination were not overtly evident, especially at the high school. Almost all the twenty-five student clubs, all the major sports teams, and all the student councils were ethnically mixed. The off-campus social clubs were discriminatory, selecting their members from the white, socially hip, male and female students. Their main activity was having parties, where maybe a little booze was consumed; they had little impact on the social life of the school. The black students kept largely to themselves but were a vital part of the school's major sports teams, and some participated in school government. George Allen, an outstanding black student with a great baritone voice, was elected senior class president. Approximately 10 percent of my graduating class of six hundred students were Latinos, but there was only one other Sanchez, and she was the beautiful one.

Living on the West Coast, being fair skinned and part of the college-bound population created a partial insulation from overt discrimination and prejudice. But I would pick up the occasional quizzical second look when my name was introduced. Once when I had a blind date and knocked on the door of the girl's home, I was amused to see her parents standing behind her, owlishly peering at me as she opened the door. I could almost hear the sigh of relief when they didn't see a brown-skinned, mustachioed lowrider, and I had to control my impulse to say *"Buenas noches."*

The high school was about three miles from Mission Hills, requiring two or three transfers on the city buses to get there. Only a few of the senior boys, either from wealthy families or hot-rod fanatics, had cars; there were none of today's gigantic parking lots for student cars. For special occasions like student dances, many of us would find a friend whose parents would let him use the car and double date. In the 1920s, my grandparents (who didn't drive) bought, at the insistence of their sons, a magnificent Packard Phaeton four-door convertible, which was accompanied with an equally magnificent Great Dane. They were gone by the time I arrived, and I didn't have a car until I was a twenty-three-year-old Marine.

Hitchhiking was far more acceptable and safer then, probably as an aftermath of the recently ended World War II, when many young servicemen on furlough would hitchhike home. In my sophomore year, when I was fifteen years old, I had a girlfriend whom I met at summer church camp and who lived in Long Beach, ninety miles north. I hitchhiked up old Highway 101 several times to visit her. Once one of my buddies and I hitchhiked to the Rose Bowl in Pasadena to cheer for our football team in the Southern California championships. In the summer after graduation, I had a very early-morning janitorial job at a Foster's Freeze ice cream store; when I was done, I would grab my swim trunks and hitchhike out to Old Mission Beach, eight miles away, to spend the day surfing and chasing girls.

I continued on my extrovert path throughout high school I ran for sophomore class president and won, and in my senior year was elected student body president—clearly signs of a promising career as an administrator. My sophomore-class grades were erratic, and I received a C in second-semester plane geometry because I was at loggerheads with the teacher over her insistence on my meticulously writing out, in two-column detail, every proof. For me, it was a waste of time. My aunt Estela saw my report card and offered me the magnificent sum of two dollars (movies were twenty-five cents then) for every A I received; I had a 4.0 average for the rest of my high-school semesters.

My disruptive behavior in class continued, but I suppose my teachers tolerated my excessive talking and being the class cutup because I was gifted, especially in mathematics. I didn't really realize this until my senior year, when I was allowed to enroll in a special honors mathematics class of twenty of the highest-achieving class "brains." Almost all of them went on to outstanding careers as engineers, lawyers, and university professors, and one received a Rhodes Scholarship. We taught ourselves trigonometry outside of class and in class raced for the answers to all kinds of problems, with the first five students to get correct ones receiving points—my kind of game!

I scored the top grade for the semester; the wonderful teacher, Mr. Kennedy, shook his head in disbelief when he informed me of my class standing. The times I spent in the principal's office as punishment must have tarnished my image.

Just before I entered high school, my grandfather left my grandmother and ran off with another woman to Mexico, where he lived until his death. With her own resources and the help of her children, my grandmother was able to keep the house and support the two of us; I did a lot of part-time jobs—mowing lawns, babysitting, and janitorial work—to earn spending money. This change meant no money for college. I had read a lot about the University of Chicago and its controversial two-year "Bastard of Arts" degree based on the Great Books curriculum, and it sounded perfect for me. A recruiter visited my high school and interviewed me, but I never heard from the university. But I eventually got there: my first job after I received my PhD was a two-year postdoctoral appointment with the University of Chicago Department of Mathematics, one of the top five math departments in the country.

CHAPTER THREE

COLLEGE
THE FIRST TWO YEARS

June 1950 and graduation arrived. I had decided to attend the local college, San Diego State College, one of the schools of the California State College (now University) System. A number of my high school classmates also attended the college, including three of my honors mathematics class "brains," who stayed for two years and then transferred to larger universities. The quality of education in the first two years of the liberal arts curriculum, as well as in mathematics, was excellent, and for fifty dollars you could pay for your semester's tuition and textbooks. My four-hundred-plus-page calculus text cost about five dollars and had at least as much information as current one-hundred-dollar texts, but didn't have multicolor graphs, pretty pictures, and a computer supplement.

It was at this time that I decided to give up the campus-popular-guy image and concentrate on intellectual pursuits, partially motivated by my reading a lot of philosophy and taking courses in economics, history, and literature. One summer I worked at a shipyard and would carry books on existentialism in my lunch pail and sometimes have a beer after work with my co-workers, which made me an okay kid. But I stuck with mathematics because I loved it and it was an easy A. I joined a fraternity, Sigma Chi, but was never a loyal, rah-rah

Greek. One of my fraternity brothers, Maynard Dunn, a very successful Yuba City businessman, is a very close, lifelong friend, but the principal benefit of membership for me was having immediate contacts through the local chapters when I transferred to another university.

My freshman English literature professor was Dr. George Phillips, a graduate of the best Ivy League universities, who remained true to his colors and wore seersucker summer suits, knit ties, and brogans to class, flaunting current California beach fashions. He was, he informed us, the second-best authority on the literature of British chimney sweeps in the world and would soon be the foremost authority, since his rival would soon pass away. He drolly pointed this out to show that the development of real expertise in a very narrow topic was the sure road to success in academia, an observation I was to later confirm.

He counseled me to move east lest I become too provincial and Southern Californian, pointing to himself as what can happen if all your higher education is centered around Cambridge, Massachusetts. He definitely encouraged a small group of his best students not to stay at San Diego State. I had little in the way of financial resources, having lost a major portion of the money I had saved for college at a wild night at the Tijuana greyhound dog-racing track, so I applied for and won a Naval ROTC (NROTC) scholarship. I traded four years of support—my junior and senior years and two years of graduate study—for three years as a commissioned officer in the Navy or Marine Corps. The scholarship required enrollment in the NROTC curriculum, wearing a uniform to weekly drills, and participating in six or eight weeks of summer training. It paid for tuition, books, and fifty dollars a month.

In the scholarship application, I had to list five universities with NROTC units that I was willing to attend. The Navy would select one of these and inform me that if I wished to receive the scholarship, this would be my school of choice. There were sixty NROTC units, located at most of the major state universities and some prestigious private ones. This forced selection had to be done to ensure that not all the candidates ended up at Harvard or Berkeley if they were intellectuals, or the University of Colorado if they wanted to ski.

In making up my list of five schools, I followed Professor Phillips's advice and selected four that were well east of the California border. But I unthinkingly added the University of New Mexico, only because one of my fraternity brothers and freshman calculus classmates had transferred there, and when he was home for the Christmas holidays, told me what a great school it was. In the spring of 1952, I was notified that I had received the scholarship and my selected school was the University of New Mexico—a real eastward move! The journey east continued later, when I applied for graduate school and my advisor suggested some Ivy League schools with prestigious mathematics departments. However, I selected the University of Michigan, which was ranked with the best. It was east enough for me!

In retrospect, I have come to realize that I am a westerner; I am happiest when I am surrounded by tall mountains, deserts, and spacious vistas, recognizing the place names left by the fur trappers, or wading a high-country trout stream. But I am also a Mexican and feel a remote kinship with Spanish-named towns and villages and like being someplace where I can hear Spanish spoken and maybe join in. I don't like to have to spell out my last name over the phone or slowly pronounce it in two distinct syllables. A little Mexican music and Mexican food now and then refreshes my spirits.

CHAPTER FOUR

NEW MEXICO
VISIT ONE

In September 1952, the Atchison, Topeka, and Santa Fe Railway delivered me and two large suitcases to the classic southwestern train station, complete with a Harvey House Hotel, in Albuquerque, New Mexico. Indians outside the station were selling curios, and I could hear some of the railroad workers speaking to each other in a Spanish that had a different nuance than mine. As I rode the bus up Central Avenue to the university, I read some of the names of the businesses—Lobo Joe's, Okies, Duran Pharmacy, the Red Barn restaurant—fascinating, slightly disorienting, and definitely not Californian. I had gotten a brief, introductory taste of the three cultures of New Mexico.

I spent the next few days in the busywork of enrollment, getting a room at Mesa Vista dormitory, checking in with the NROTC unit to get sworn in and draw my uniforms, and registering for classes. Registering caused my first problem, because the registrar insisted that I had to major in some subject, and I told her I wanted to continue my quest of being the last great Renaissance man. She didn't think this was funny; we argued for a while and finally agreed on mathematics.

"Now what about a minor? With mathematics as a major, a minor in the sciences, such as chemistry or physics, would be appropriate," she declared.

"Never!" I responded. "It's too narrow. Let's make it philosophy."

I tried to explain to her that I was continuing the fine tradition set by Alfred North Whitehead and Bertrand Russell in England, but failed. In New Mexico, Californians were regarded as a little quirky, and I was keeping up our reputation.

Albuquerque is bordered on the west by the Rio Grande and on the east by the Sandia Mountains (10,000 ft. elevation). The fabled Route 66 crosses it from Gallup headed toward Amarillo. Before the semester began, I rode the bus downtown to look around; the city population was about one hundred thousand, and it would be many years before the suburban blight set in. There were two movie houses, the classic Alvarado Hotel, some medium-size department stores, and some shops that sold Indian pottery, Navajo rugs, cowboy hats and belts, and guns. Some of the restaurants served enchiladas, even with an egg on top (strange!). I was going to have to make some dietary adjustments, since Madre Cons rarely prepared Mexican food, except for big batches of tamales for family parties.

In the local newspaper and on advertisements, I would see names like mine, which pleased me, and familiar names, like Chavez and Martinez. But there were different ones, too, like Archuleta, Baca, and Vigil, and references to things Spanish or Hispanic, a new word for me; the word "Mexican" was never used to refer to things New Mexican, and sometimes even had a pejorative flavor. In my family Spanish was the language we spoke, but the Spanish tyrants were kicked out of Mexico in 1821 and were not spoken of kindly, even though we prided ourselves on the blend of Indian and Spanish that made up the great Mexican culture, often called "*La raza cósmica*." In the interests of civility, when asked, I would just say I came from California.

The University of New Mexico had about forty-five hundred students enrolled, many from influential Anglo families of the state. It had excellent academic programs, especially in anthropology and Latin American studies. During my stay, two Rhodes Scholars were selected from its undergraduates. Its neighboring rival, the University of Arizona, which is now a major research university, was not as good then. In Southern California in those days, if you were rich and smart you went to Stanford; if you were poor and smart you went to the University of California, Berkeley; if you were rich and wanted to party you went to the University of Southern California; if you were poor and wanted to party you went to the University of Arizona.

I got a room in the dorm and a roommate who was never around. I found myself largely surrounded by young men who wore to class boots, Levi's, cowboy shirts, and wide belts with a rodeo buckle commemorating the conquest of some wild steer or rebellious horse. While the climate was warm, I wore my California faded blue denims and Hawaiian shirts, which didn't elicit too much comment, but I narrowly missed a fight one evening when I asked a student coming down the hall in his finest Western regalia if he had a date with a cow. To help stretch my fifty-dollar stipend, I worked for my meals by hashing (serving meals and washing dishes) at some sorority houses.

I started classes, which included a yearlong NROTC class on naval battles. Because there were so few mathematics majors, almost all my mathematics courses were in the evening, from six thirty to quarter to eight, or eight to quarter past nine, or both, to take advantage of evening students, mostly engineers from Kirtland Air Force Base and affiliated laboratories. They were a humorless bunch that took copious notes and carried briefcases; some had slide rules in holsters strapped to their belts. After a day of other classes, NROTC drills, hashing three meals, some studying, and a little goofing off, it was tough facing those evening classes. They made a dent in my social life, but I didn't have much money or a car, so it didn't have that much of an impact, especially since the curfew for all women living in dormitories and sorority houses was 10:00 p.m.

The philosophy department had only two faculty, Professors Alexander and Bahm, and one graduate assistant, who wore sandals with soles cut out from bicycle tires and no socks—a hippie before his time. I had never encountered a philosopher before, except in my reading, and it was fascinating for me to observe their mental processes. I finally decided that they were like mathematicians, only working from sets of axioms different from Euclid's.

My second semester I was accepted as a transfer member of the local chapter of Sigma Chi and decided to move from the dormitory to the fraternity house—it was cheaper and would improve my social life. A number of the members were NROTC students from out of state: the only Hispanic was an outstanding athlete from Santa Rosa. But there was one member who was a loyal Southern Californian and had a snazzy convertible, so it was never a problem getting home on semester breaks or even on long weekends if there was a party going on. Eight hundred miles, at fifty-five miles an hour, on the two-lane Route 66 and you were back to the Promised Land. On one trip we decided to see the Grand Canyon. We drove up to the rim, got out of the car, looked for a couple of minutes, and briefly commented on its size, then continued our breakneck journey home. Party time!

In the summer of my junior year, I was required to go on an eight-week summer training cruise to Santos, Brazil; Cartagena, Colombia; and our base at Guantanamo, Cuba, on the

USS *Albany*, a heavy cruiser leaving from Norfolk, Virginia. Three of us had a car, so we decided to drive there; on the trip I was dramatically introduced to racism. We had a minor automobile repair problem and stopped at a Sears garage in Little Rock, Arkansas. I asked one of the mechanics where the men's bathroom was, and he pointed over his shoulder toward the back of the garage. I saw a door and headed toward it when he cursed and yelled, "No! Not that one!" and pointed toward a nearby door. The first door was marked Colored Only. Filled with shock and anger, I returned to my companions and said, "Let's get the hell out of here as soon as we can." The memory of that incident has stayed with me all these years.

While we waited in non-air-conditioned barracks to go aboard ship, and also during the cruise steaming across the equator in July, I came to the conclusion that I *hated* humidity—not heat but humidity. This reinforced my loyalty to the West. In the last week of the cruise I saw a young ensign whom I had not seen during the previous seven weeks. I asked one of the petty officers who he was. The reply was that he was the junior engineering officer and that he spent most of his time in the inferno-like engine room, deep in the bowels of the ship. I decided that this would surely be my fate if I accepted a Navy appointment, which stimulated my decision to be commissioned in the Marine Corps.

We got to spend four days in Santos, where between Spanish and English I could piece together Portuguese. I managed to get myself invited to an exclusive beach resort by a family whose lovely daughter I tried to convince to come to the United States to study physics. In Cartagena I was right in my element and two or three of my shipmates always wanted to tag along. We spent some time seated on benches in the City Plaza enjoying the well-chaperoned young ladies' eye-flirting as they strolled by. Their brothers or male cousins were close by looking daggers; we just had to make sure they weren't carrying machetes. Guantanamo was a treat, and although we were not allowed off the base, I could go to the Post Exchange soda fountain to have my beloved chocolate malt and grilled cheese sandwich.

I hitchhiked and rode the bus from Norfolk to San Diego and spent several weeks with Madre Cons. She was living alone, and although my uncles watched over her, she was lonely. I was an awful correspondent because although I read and spoke Spanish fluently, my writing was terrible—accent marks are a curse! During my first semester away, my grandmother once called the dean of the university to complain that I wasn't writing home. I got called on the carpet, which was very embarrassing. While I was home Madre Cons would fix my favorite breakfast: two fried eggs and bacon, covered over with frijoles, and flour tortillas. It still hits the spot like no other breakfast.

I returned to the campus for my senior year to face the terrible ordeal of satisfying the foreign-language requirement, two semesters at the second-year level. I had taken two years of German in high school and didn't like it, but signed up for advanced German. I received a first-semester grade of D but improved the second semester to a D+. This would not have been possible without the help of my roommate, Bob Wertheim, son of a prominent German merchant family from Fort Sumner, who also took the course. He was a firm taskmaster, but we have been close friends ever since. People used to ask me why I took German instead of Spanish, which would have been a cinch. I guess it was because I felt it would not be a challenge. If you are a science or mathematics major, taking French or German is recommended; I took the required German exam in graduate school and have not read one word of German since.

Besides German, I had to take an upper-division course in the humanities, so I elected an advanced course in the neoclassical period of English literature. It was awful, and the only thing I remember from it is the definition of the word "hudibrastic." My grade point average took a tumble. Some of the reason for this was that I was spending a lot of time reading philosophy. The end result was that I was one class hour short of graduation, thereby finishing in the class of 1955 instead of 1954. I made up the hour by writing a paper on ballistics during my summer training cruise and was admitted into the graduate program in mathematics.

At the start of the semester, I met a beautiful freshman girl, Margaret Vigil, from Clayton, New Mexico, and fell very much in love. Several times, I rode the bus or hitchhiked the 270 miles north to visit her during vacations, and no matter what time I arrived, by the next morning the town knew that Margaret's beau was in town. On one of my hitchhiking trips I was picked up by a couple of tipsy drifters who were swigging red wine between the big towns so that they could "reinvigorate" their blood and sell it to get gas money. To save on gas, whenever they came to the top of a grade they would cut off the engine and coast to the bottom in neutral gear. I bailed out at Springer.

Margaret was Hispanic, lived in one of the dormitories, and was not pledged to one of the sororities, all of which was of no importance to me. I brought her to the fraternity dances and parties, recognizing that they really were fraternity-sorority events and Margaret didn't fit in. The sororities were all Anglo, and the condescending, snobbish way some of their campus queens greeted or conversed with or just ignored Margaret was awful. She never said anything about it, but I know she was hurt, and so was I. Our relationship lasted until the spring, when Margaret decided to quit school. During the summer she came to Albuquerque several times to visit relatives, and we saw each other, but clearly it was all over.

I started thinking about my name again. Was I accepted by my fraternity brothers because I looked Anglo, was a previous member of Sigma Chi at San Diego State, and kept my Mexicanness to myself? Was this the reason the sorority girls were willing to go on dates with me? Why did none of my fraternity brothers date some of the beautiful Hispanic girls? I began to understand what it felt like to be of Mexican parentage and not fit the stereotype—when it mattered and when it didn't. The social upheavals of the seventies, the Chicano Movement, and affirmative action changed all that.

The summer came, and I had a month before starting my summer training, so I needed a job and some money. The father of one of my fraternity brothers was a civil engineer in Palm Springs, so his son and I surveyed lots in Desert Hot Springs, which was then nothing but desert. It was a great job; we would get up at dawn, get our instruments, and go to work. Since the survey instruments were optical, by noon it was too hot for them to be accurate. So we would quit work, buy some beer, and find a swimming pool and some girls. In those days before air-conditioning, Palm Springs in the summer was a quiet, pleasant California desert town, too hot for the tourists, golfers, and Hollywood celebrities.

The summer training took place for three weeks in Little Creek, Virginia, for amphibious training (and more humidity), followed by three weeks in Corpus Christi, Texas, for Naval Air training (and a little less humidity). During the aviation training we were each given a demonstration flight in a two-seated training plane. I asked my pilot to put the plane through all the paces to see if I liked aviation. He said he was not allowed to do that, but I was insistent and he craved some variety, so we flew over the King Ranch, and for ten minutes I had no idea where the horizon was. I thanked him when we returned and definitely decided on the Marine Corps.

One Sunday in Corpus Christi, the New Mexico NROTC unit had the duty, so we were restricted to the base for the day. We were all pretty bored, when I remembered that there were a lot of jack rabbits on the big, empty fields on the base. We decided to organize what we called a New Mexico Indian rabbit hunt. We stripped down to swimming trunks and tennis shoes, and maybe some cowboy hats, found a field with some rabbits, formed a big circle around one of them, and started closing the circle, yelling and screaming in what we thought were suitable Indian hunting cries. There were about twenty of us, so it was pretty noisy and drew some attention from some of the officers' houses adjoining the field. As the circle closed, the rabbit would panic and finally try to break through, when one of us would grab it, do a victory dance holding the rabbit aloft, and then let the poor creature go. Unfortunately, the base commander, an admiral, was having a cocktail party on his patio, which his guests deserted and went to watch the rabbit hunt over the fence. We received a reprimand the next day from our commanding officer, who couldn't help smiling once in awhile.

In the fall, I moved out of the fraternity and its bedlam and got a room and meals in the house of the Ike Singer family, about a mile from campus. They had three school-age boys, and my job was to be home when they got out of school, help them with their homework, and do some babysitting if Ike and his wife wanted to go out. This helped a lot with my studies—I took two advanced mathematics courses, the required third-year NROTC course, which was a Marine Corps course on the history of warfare, and an upper-division course on ancient, pre-Roman history. I got all As; there were no Graduate Record Exams in those days, so maybe with those grades and what must have been positive letters from my professors, I was admitted to graduate study at the University of Michigan.

In early January of 1955, I put on my NROTC uniform, packed a suitcase with cold-weather clothes, went to Kirtland Air Force Base, and hitched a space-available flight to Chanute

Air Force Base, Illinois. From there I took the bus to Ann Arbor, Michigan, where I had made arrangements to stay at the Sigma Chi house until I could find a room. I arrived at midnight on a cold winter evening; when I took my first steps out of the bus station, I fell flat on my rear end—we didn't have icy sidewalks in Albuquerque.

CHAPTER FIVE

ANN ARBOR
VISIT ONE

Everything at the University of Michigan was big: the stadium that held ninety thousand spectators; the three-story Student Union, with its guest rooms, lounges, and basement cafeteria; Angell Hall, the city-block-long, four-story building whose whole third floor held the mathematics department with more than forty faculty; the law school, modeled after an Oxford college; the huge main library, which was the focal point of a beautiful quadrangle surrounded by classroom buildings. Then there were the football players, midwestern giants like I had never seen before. Some were members of Sigma Chi, the most notable being the affable All American end and NFL standout Ron Kramer.

Surrounded and awestruck by all this immensity, which dwarfed any school I had ever seen, I found my own little, comfortable niche. I rented a room with a bed, dresser, desk, and shared bathroom in a rooming house near campus and arranged for my meals at the fraternity house. This gave me some parties to go to and some social contacts, although mathematics majors are always regarded as coming from some other planet even farther than exotic New Mexico. I did miss speaking Spanish but found a fellow student from Puerto Rico who was studying statistics. We would have coffee together twice a week. He spoke Puerto Rican Spanish and I spoke Mexican Spanish, so our informal conversation was frequently, but cordially, one-sided. Nevertheless we greatly enjoyed babbling at each other about our academic lives and plans. The mathematics department had its own library and that is where I spent much of my time.

I had arrived in January, and the coeds were outfitted in their winter garb—hats, scarves, heavy sweaters and parkas, wool skirts, and knitted socks that went beyond the knee. A sign of spring was the welcome appearance of ankles. I thought that most of the undergraduates were midwestern, until I overheard one girl turn to her companion and ask her if she wanted to go get a cup of "kawhfee"—the dreaded East was nearby! I found out later that the University of Michigan was very popular with New Yorkers who hadn't made the cut at the Ivy League schools.

The mathematics courses I took were mostly in applied mathematics and largely depended on having excellent computational skills and a strong background in calculus, both of which I had. The master's degree candidates were not important to the professors: you were required to take some introductory graduate courses and maybe one or two electives. The MS and MA degrees were basically regarded as trade degrees for persons who were going into industry or teaching in small colleges.

Summer training time came, and I spent six weeks at the Marine Corps schools in Quantico, Virginia—humidity again! The training was a modified form of boot camp, with very sharp enlisted men as drill instructors, who frequently had a hard time handling platoons of wise-ass college students. I sometimes thought they were a little extra tough because we might be their commanding officers in the future. Maybe they were getting even ahead of time. The summer experience, physical and tactical training, spit and polish, and watching the creation of the fabled Marine Corps esprit de corps, definitely convinced me that I had made the right decision in becoming a gung ho future Marine.

Fall in Michigan and the Big Ten Conference were unforgettable experiences for me, with football being the dominant theme and the fall colors the backdrop. I went to one game in November and was amazed to see ninety thousand redcheeked fans cheering and jumping up and down while their toes were certainly turning blue. Not for me. I always try to watch the Michigan–Ohio State game on TV at home or at a gathering of local Michigan alumni. I contribute to the mathematics scholarship funds at New Mexico and Michigan, but my sports loyalties are with Michigan.

Studies were not going well, and it was because my mathematics education was lacking two essential ingredients: a strong theoretical foundation and the ability to construct a formal proof of a mathematical statement. Being able to do a complicated calculation had taken me as far as I could go, and my limitation caught up with me—one professor questioned why I had been admitted to the graduate program. Compounded with this was my emotional immaturity and my questioning what my goals in life were and what my career would be. All this took its toll. I decided to stop my graduate program early, five hours short of a master's degree and requested an early commissioning, not waiting until June. A career as a Marine Corps officer seemed a strong possibility.

I finished the fall semester with satisfactory grades, went home for several months, and was commissioned at the NROTC unit at the University of Southern California in March 1956. Then I left for Basic School, Quantico, to begin Officers Basic Class 2–56.

CHAPTER SIX

SEMPER FI
THE FIRST YEAR

I checked in at Mainside, the central headquarters in the town of Quantico, and was shuttled six miles to my home for twenty-six weeks, Camp Upshur. A Quonset hut enclave with a big, asphalt parade field, it was located in the middle of the steamy Virginia forest—full of chiggers, ticks, copperheads, and humidity. In 1996, when I visited Quantico for a reunion, the Basic School had moved to Mainside and the candidates were housed in modern, air-conditioned apartment buildings. This allowed me to tell some of them that we had it rougher in the "Old Corps"—a much used and sometimes humorous expression referring to the time *you* served, and not to the days of canvas leggings and Springfield rifles.

The first job was drawing what was called 782 Gear—green dungaree shirts and pants, combat boots, canteens, entrenching tools, mess kits, camp stools (for long, outdoor lectures), and big, heavy ponchos (for staying dry outside and wet inside while sitting through long, outdoor lectures). All this stuff and more made up the thirty-plus-pound pack that we had to carry on marches into the boondocks, along with a nine-and-a-half-pound M-1 rifle and bayonet. We knew that as officers, we would be issued a pistol and probably never have to carry a rifle, but our training was as infantrymen, not officers.

The next task was to get measured by some Washington, D.C./Quantico military haberdasher for dress uniforms: tan for summer and green for winter. I had a regular commission, so was also required to purchase dress whites, presumably for guard duty at some Middle Eastern embassy, and dress blues, which I might wear if I got White House duty. They were very expensive; I never wore the whites and wore the blues once at a Marine Corps birthday party.

The then-commandant of the Marine Corps was a clothes freak, so regular officers were also required to purchase a huge, green wool, Prussian-style overcoat, perfect for Yukon duty (I dodged this one), and gloves, which were *never* to be worn. They were carried in the left hand, wrapped around a swagger stick, which was a dark brown, eighteen-inch, leather-covered stick; some candidates purchased ebony ones with silver tips. I never knew its real purpose, but an ex-Navy commander friend said it was to keep the dogs from peeing on your leg when you were standing at attention.

Next was a run to the nearest Post Exchange to purchase all the cleaning gear we would need: laundry soap, metal polish to shine belt buckles and all the collar and shoulder lieutenant bars and ornaments, and cordovan shoe polish. Our dress shoes had to be spit shined by dipping a cloth in the polish, then in a container (usually the shoe-polish lid) of water, then rubbing it on the shoe in a circular motion, a little bit at a time. Diligent applications, maybe taking three or four hours, would produce a mirror-like finish one could shave by. Some fanatics even spit shined their combat boots.

Then there were all the oils and solvents needed to clean our rifles; a blemish on a shoe might be tolerated, but a speck on a rifle barrel was sure to result in a dressing down. We joked about this: "A clean rifle means a clean mind." We purchased soaps and brushes to scrub our field gear, and irons to press our dress uniforms—good training for prospective valets.

The philosophy of the Basic School was that every Marine Corps officer, no matter what his eventual mission might be—tank commander, aviator, forward observer, supply officer, and so forth—was first trained to be an infantry officer and to lead a platoon in combat if needed. We took introductory classes and had demonstrations in many military specialties but the basic training focused on infantry tactics and teamwork. I think this accounts for the tremendous esprit de corps the Marine Corps is famous for.

There were two companies in the 2–56 Basic Class, Charlie Company and mine, Delta Company, each with 142 officer candidates. There were no blacks in the class and only one other Latino, a Cuban American from Florida in Charlie Company. Delta Company had thirteen ex-enlisted officers, older men of the rank of sergeant and above who had been selected to be commissioned officers and were sometimes called "mustangs." Several had served at the end of World War II. They were a little bothered at first by training and taking classes with a bunch of wise-ass college graduates who were not so awed by rank, but by the end of the class, we were all very close, had benefited much from their wisdom, and had enjoyed their stories.

The company commanding officer was Major "Locker Box" Jones—we never found out where the nickname came from—who was an ex-enlisted man and had had meritorious service in the Pacific campaigns of World War II and the Korean War. I think he was uncomfortable with college graduates and favored the ex-enlisted candidates when it came to the rotating leadership assignments we took on while training. Neither he nor my platoon commanding officer, Captain Pierson, an Aggie from Texas, seemed to be quite comfortable with a candidate named Sánchez who had advanced training in mathematics.

Our accommodations were Quonset huts; they were not air-conditioned and had interiors that were arranged in two long rows of bunk beds. Each of us was assigned one narrow wall locker and one footlocker for all our uniforms and gear, which had to be specially arranged as specified in some manual. We were given instructions on how to make our beds so that a quarter would bounce off it; anyone who came back from class and found his bed torn apart knew he had gotten an F in bed making that day. I shared my bunk with Sal Scarpato, an Italian American graduate of the University of Maine from Union City, New Jersey. His upbringing in a working-class home, where no English was spoken, was similar to mine. We shared the same philosophy—that a sense of humor had to be maintained to survive the training. This did not endear us to our commanding officers, and we have been close friends for life.

The officers who were our instructors in the many classes we took—tactics, weaponry, logistics, military law, mapping, intelligence—had obviously been especially selected. They were sharp and well-educated captains, majors, and colonels, many of whom were later decorated for their service in Vietnam; I would see their names in newsclips. Their example made it easy to consider a Marine Corps career, and I had that seriously in mind when I left Basic School.

After twenty-six weeks of training with memories of lots of heat and lots of mud, I was assigned an artillery specialty; the hot dogs in the class all aspired for infantry assignments and some were crushed when they didn't get them. So I spent four more weeks in Quantico taking an artillery course and having the luxury of living in officers' quarters. Then I was given orders to report to Camp Pendleton, California, for assignment to the 12th Marines, an artillery regiment stationed in Gotemba, Japan, at the base of Mount Fujiyama. On the drive back to the West Coast, I stopped in Ciudad Juárez to spend an evening with Padre Cecilio, who was living there with his lady companion. She prepared a wonderful dinner, and we drank a lot. On the walk back to the border, he insisted that we stop at a local cantina and have a few drinks with some of his friends. Afterward, he accompanied me to the border-crossing bridge; I staggered across and barely made it to my car, where I collapsed until the next morning. I was sure that my grandfather, sixty years older than me, had probably stopped on the way back and had a nightcap. That was the last time I saw him.

I drove to Camp Pendleton, California, had some time to spend in San Diego with Madre Cons, then flew from San Francisco to Japan in a Lockheed Constellation prop plane, and reported to the Yokosuka Naval Base. For a few days, I recovered from the plane trip and did the necessary paperwork, assuming I would be given transportation to my new assignment. But RHIP (Rank Has Its Privileges) did not apply to lowly lieutenants—I was handed a train ticket to Gotemba and given a ride to the train station. I could not read Japanese and there were no translations of the station names, so I might have ended up in Vladivostok if it hadn't been for the help of a kind Scandinavian minister who traveled with me. My career in the Fleet Marine Force started off with a little divine guidance.

CHAPTER SEVEN

SEMPER FI
SAYONARA

The 12th Marine Regiment was the artillery arm of the 3rd Marine Division, all stationed in Japan and later in Okinawa. The standard tour of duty was fourteen months with no dependents allowed, and except for emergencies, no leaves back to the United States to visit families. The rationale for this was that the Marines had to be combat ready at the first sound of gunfire west of Hawaii. It didn't seem much of a hardship to me, but I was disturbed when one evening at the Officers' Club, several married senior officers, who should have been setting the example, began recruiting a group to go into town and see "the ladies." The model set by my instructors at Basic School began to get tarnished.

After three months in Japan, the entire division, comprising three infantry regiments, one artillery regiment, and all the logistic and supply personnel, moved to the north end of the island of Okinawa, which is located in the Ryukyu chain of islands south of Japan. The only major city is Naha, but we were stationed out in the boondocks. It was back to Quonset huts and metal-sided temporary buildings, but at least the Officers' Club, a flattering nomenclature, had a swimming pool and a senior sergeant club manager who was a genius at scrounging up good liquor and French wines. For the lieutenants, his coup was finding quite a few tar-covered cases of Pabst beer somewhere in World War II salvage. We formed the Ten-Cents Pabst Club, which lasted until the beer ran out.

The no-dependents status for the Marines was made more difficult by the presence of Sukiran Army Base and Kadena Air Force Base in the central part of the island. Both had sizeable adjoining family residential areas for the officers with all the amenities of home, including wives, children, and automobiles. Kadena had a plush Officers' Club, with a restaurant, bar, and a ballroom with an orchestra for weekend dancing. Marine Corps officers were only begrudgingly allowed admittance because they often got drunk and started fights, partially out of frustration. We were considered the Animal House of the island.

I was assigned a howitzer battery. My company commander, a captain, was making sure he would get promoted to the rank of major and get a nice pension after twenty years of service. If a captain didn't get promoted he would receive an honorable discharge and have to leave the service. "Not on my watch" was the going philosophy—no screw ups. If things went well the captain gave himself the credit, but if something went wrong, it was the lieutenants' fault. He called me Speedy, referring to the Speedy Gonzalez jokes ("Wham! Bam! Thank you, Ma'am!"), and I hated it.

We called the battalion commander "The Coach"; he was a major who had played football for North Carolina. Unfortunately, that was about the level of his leadership qualities. He refused to acknowledge that the young enlisted men were adults and should be treated as such. I got into several arguments with him over whether it was okay for the men to stay up after lights out at 10:00 p.m. to read, write letters, or clean their field gear. The conversation got pretty heated when I mentioned that nowhere in my training had I been given instructions on how to tuck in my troops.

All of this began to weigh heavily on me. Three months after I arrived overseas, I wrote the University of Michigan and informed them that I would be back in 1959 to complete my master's degree. In retrospect, I recognize that my three years in the Marine Corps were needed, maturing me and helping me see my future more clearly, while developing my leadership skills and an understanding of chain of command that would be valuable later on. I am proud to have been a member of the Corps.

While I was in Okinawa, the entire division was put on ships and landed in the Philippines in its eastern jungles, where we engaged in a major exercise maneuvering against an imaginary enemy. The only threatening rustling we heard in the undergrowth was local natives scuttling around selling San Miguel beer. Several months later, we were awakened at midnight, ordered to put on full combat gear, and put aboard ship. We cruised around the western Pacific for several days but were never told why. Our supply officer mentioned that he had real difficulties obtaining boxes of diapers and sanitary napkins, so we assumed that our mission had been to help evacuate U.S. civilians, probably from Cambodia, where there had been some flare-ups.

Two wonderful things happened to me while I was stationed in Okinawa. I was selected for the Regimental Rifle and Pistol Team, which in January 1958 would be shipped to Hawaii, with additional temporary pay for four months to train for the division matches in May. But more important was that in June 1957, I met my future wife, Joan Thomas, at an Officers' Club party where some single girls on the island, mostly officers' daughters home from school, were brave enough to face the "animals." Joan was the daughter of Colonel Lucius Thomas, an Army medical officer assigned to the Ryukus government, and Ruth Thomas. She had just graduated from college and was planning to work on the island as an Army civilian.

When Joan walked into the club, I was at the welcome table, tipsily handing out corsages of pink-colored flowers. I offered her one, but she declined, stating that pink flowers did not go with her orange dress.

"Miss Thomas, you must know that in the last issue of *Vogue*, Christian Dior stated that pink and orange would be the fashion colors of the Paris season."

Pure baloney, but it worked, and she took a corsage, looking at me a little strangely. When I entered the dining room my luck was still running, because the only empty chair was next to Joan. I told her of my plans to go back to Michigan. She must have thought I was a little weird—a Marine Corps officer who was going to study mathematics and knew about Paris fashion. But she agreed to go with me after the party to an interservice baseball game, and our courtship began.

The Thomas family had a lovely home in the officers' housing, two maids, and a car, and they provided great home cooking with a Southern flavor. I would spend the weekends with them when I could, go to movies and interservice baseball games, and then take a late Sunday night bus back to my quarters. The ride was long; Okinawan buses had no interior lights, so I amused myself and stayed awake by mentally computing squares of integers up to 100, which is easy—for example, $72 \times 72 = (70 + 2) \times (70 + 2) = 4{,}900 + (2 \times 2 \times 70) + 4 = 5{,}184$.

After a courtship of six months, during which I was away two months on maneuvers and training, Joan and I were married at the Sukiran Army Base church in a full military wedding. The regimental commanding officer, Colonel Kramer, insisted that Joan and I ride off on top of a 4.5-inch rocket launcher. In the Old Corps, artillery officers and their brides rode off from the ceremony on a caisson, a wheeled vehicle used to carry ammunition. These no longer existed. Afterward, I left for Hawaii, and Joan, who was now a Marine Corps dependent, had to return to the United States. She boarded a military flight to San Francisco, but when it landed in Hawaii an officer came aboard and regretfully informed her that her seat was assigned to a senior officer, and she had to be bumped from the flight. We never found out who arranged that, but we had a wonderful four-month honeymoon in a small cottage at Ewa Beach, near the rifle range, courtesy of the Marine Corps.

My last assignment before being discharged was division education officer for the First Marine Division, stationed at Camp Pendleton, which gave Joan an opportunity to get to know my family. We arrived in San Diego by train and the whole Sánchez crew, Mexican sombreros and all, was there to greet us—the arrival of a new bride in a Mexican family is a big event. From the train station we went to the family home and were greeted at the door by the wedding march resounding from the player grand piano; then came the drinks, food, and hugs. Joan, who was following Anglo protocol and keeping secret the fact that she was three-months pregnant, was overwhelmed. Madre Cons quickly figured that out the next morning, when Joan, faced with the smell of a plateful of refried beans and fried eggs, had to leave the table abruptly.

I got the assignment at Camp Pendleton because the previous holder, who had served with me in Okinawa, had recommended me on the strength of my academic background. The division education officer reported directly to the division commander, Lieutenant General Snedeker, and was a member of his staff. My responsibility was to monitor every unit's educational activities, including checking enrollment in correspondence courses and the local junior college, and most importantly, encouraging those enlisted men who did not have a high-school diploma to study for and take the GED exams. It was my kind of job. When I informed the general in March 1959 of my decision to return to the university, I was flattered when he took some time to discuss my plans with me, even offering to write a letter of recommendation if I needed one. It was a nice way to leave the Corps.

From the above narrative you can tell that, aside from the repulsive Speedy Gonzalez moniker, my last name was of no consequence, to my knowledge, during my year and a half in graduate school and three years in the Marine Corps. My Mexican roots and my bilingualism played no role in my achievements; I was just another lieutenant and just another student. That suited me just fine.

CHAPTER EIGHT

ANN ARBOR
VISIT TWO

Joan and I and three-month-old Bruce, born at the naval hospital at Camp Pendleton in 1959, drove to San Francisco to stay with her parents until I started school. Colonel Thomas was chief medical officer at the historic Presidio in San Francisco; his quarters were a huge, two-story house on a hill overlooking the Presidio, so there was room for us. I spent four months refreshing my mathematics, walking around the Marina District, and, in the basement, building a lovely little fly rod that I still use on smaller streams. We decided that I would go back to Michigan by myself, finish up my required courses in summer school, and then come back to the West Coast and look for a job. In June 1959, I rode the bus to Ann Arbor, got a room in a graduate dormitory with two crazy University of South Dakota librarians as my neighbors, and returned to Angell Hall.

While in summer school I thought that staying in Ann Arbor for another year or two and taking some more mathematics courses to improve my job opportunities was a good idea. This required getting an income that would support me and my family. Since I hadn't applied for a teaching assistantship, I looked for employment at one of the research laboratories of the university. It turned out, to my surprise, that my

Marine Corps experience and my mathematics degrees were very attractive to an operations research group at the university's Willow Run Laboratories, later to become the Institute of Science and Technology.

The group was doing kind of wacky, large-scale, combat simulations for the Army, and since none of the scientists had any military experience, they thought I could contribute to their research. Computer capabilities in those days were primitive, relying largely on input from punched cards. But I could put colored tacks representing enemy and friendly units on maps as well as anybody, so I got the job. It paid $6,000 a year, and students could take up to two courses a semester as long as they made up the time spent on campus. Once I had a job, I went back to San Francisco, picked up Joan and Bruce, and we drove to Ann Arbor. At first we moved into the married-student housing complex, but later moved into the upstairs apartment of a house two blocks away from the football stadium. My graduate career had begun!

While I was in summer school, I took an advanced algebra course from Professor Jack McLaughlin, who was fearsome. He would snuff out his cigarette just before entering class, then go to the blackboard, pick up the chalk, start writing definitions and theorems at a breakneck speed for fifty minutes without notes, return the chalk, and walk out the door. His exams were nearly impossible, but I managed to get a B for the class. After I received it, I stopped by his office to ask how that grade would affect my standing in the graduate program. His response helped guide the rest of my time at Michigan.

"Sánchez, the department doesn't give a damn about your grades; it just demands that you write a thesis of Michigan quality."

Life as a married graduate student was pleasant and very simple. On the weekday mornings I would car pool or drive out to the lab, which was eight miles from campus, and return later if I had a class. Joan would be busy with her activities; if it was a nice fall afternoon, she would put Bruce in the stroller and join other graduate students' wives and children at one of the athletic practice fields and watch the stupendous Michigan Marching Band. On the weekends we might go for a picnic or invite another graduate couple over, bunk any children in a bedroom, make some popcorn, open some beer, and play bridge. I resumed my boyhood interest in chess and would play at the local club once a week and in nearby tournaments.

During the year I took a course from Professor Douglas Dickson that was supposed to be on integration theory. Instead, to my benefit, he decided to spend most of the semester on the foundations of analysis, which filled in the gaps that I had experienced when I first attended Michigan. I took a few more advanced courses, then one day the graduate student advisor called me in to suggest I take the PhD preliminary exams. This came as a surprise, since my plans did not include working toward a doctorate; I was just enjoying working at the lab, where I was a staff member, doing analysis in the Radar Group, and taking courses or seminars. I talked the idea over with Joan, and we decided "Why not?" There was nothing to lose if I flunked.

There were two exams, one in algebra and one in analysis, and in those days they were oral exams. Candidates were told to appear at 7:00 p.m. at the department; each was assigned to a faculty office whose door was closed. The candidate entered, found two faculty members seated at the desks and was told to go to the blackboard and pick up some chalk. Then the questioning began and continued for one hour. It could be pretty brutal. The second exam would be taken a few days later. Shortly after that the candidate would be informed of the results by the graduate advisor. Some students who didn't pass had spent hours memorizing statements of theorems and their proofs, but their examiners had selected, instead, some elementary mathematical property like continuity, asking for a complete development of it and its implications. I passed the exams.

Next came the matter of finding a faculty member to direct my PhD research and dissertation writing. I was taking a class in variational methods from a world-class analyst, Professor Lamberto Cesari, and in my work at the Radar Group had come across a problem that could be approached using some of the methods developed in his class. I suggested the problem to Professor Cesari, he thought it was a good idea and agreed to be my advisor. I went to work. A year later, with the professor demanding weekly progress, the dissertation was written—its title was "Calculus of Variations for Integrals Depending on a Convolution Product." Sounds pretty impressive but I didn't get on the Nobel Prize short list.

In those days there was the requirement that every PhD candidate take two language examinations. Each consisted of a general grammar and vocabulary screening test, which was a real killer, followed by translating, in front of an examiner, a passage from a technical work that you could select. The language choices for mathematics students were French, German, and Russian. However, since Professor Cesari was very influential, and I was reading a lot of Italian research papers, I was allowed to substitute Italian, which was a piece of cake. But then came German, which had a fearsome reputation. One very bright student who later became a mathematics professor at a major university flunked the screening exam six times and was finally given an honorary pass.

My strategy for passing the German screening exam was a simple but laborious one: I reviewed the first six chapters of an elementary grammar book, and then spent a month memorizing every card in a one-thousand-word vocabulary box. The screening test was multiple choice, and I had no problem with the vocabulary part. When I came to the grammar part,

I either knew the answer or could usually narrow it down to two choices. When I had to make a choice, I would take a half dollar out of my pocket and flip it to decide which answer to select. I heard a few gasps from the other examinees, and the exam proctor sneered at me, but I passed the exam.

As I wrote my dissertation and spent time talking to my advisor and other professors, I realized that I was being drawn inexorably to consider a life as an academic—teaching and doing research at some college or university. It didn't seem a bad idea. I figured that if I could stand in front of a skeptical audience and do magic tricks, I could teach a calculus class to largely unappreciative students. At a summer mathematics association meeting, I met some nice faculty from Oregon State University. It looked like a good school to consider, especially noting the fact that Oregon had great fishing. In the spring of 1963, I applied for a position and assumed that in the fall I would be in Corvallis, Oregon, or exploring some neighboring trout stream. But I hadn't accounted for the backroom negotiations of my advisor and the eminent expositor and mathematician Professor Paul Halmos.

Professor Halmos liked to practice his Spanish. There were no other Spanish speakers on the faculty or among the graduate students, so whenever he encountered me, we would have a brief, friendly conversation in Spanish. One spring day we ran into each other on the quad walking toward Angell Hall, and he asked me what my plans were. I mentioned Oregon State. He seemed very surprised, but I didn't think anything about it until several days later, when I received a call at the lab from Professor Irving Kaplansky, chair of the University of Chicago Department of Mathematics and one of the world's giants of mathematics. My reaction might be compared to the village priest receiving a call from the Pope or the bush-league third baseman getting one from Tommy Lasorda.

Professor Kaplansky chatted with me for a few minutes and then offered me one of five two-year postdoctoral instructorships at the University of Chicago Department of Mathematics, long regarded as one of the top mathematics departments in the country. I was staggered, because I didn't think I was in that league, but I accepted. I found out later how the offer came about. After our conversation on the quad, Professor Halmos, who had recently been on the faculty of the University of Chicago, rushed up to Professor Cesari's office. The two of them decided that they couldn't possibly send me to what they regarded as the mathematical hinterlands, so they called Kaplansky. He checked me out, and then made the call.

Early in the summer, Joan and I drove the 240 miles to the south side of Chicago to look over our new home, a three-story brownstone apartment building at Fifty-Fifth and Ingleside, owned by the mathematics department and used for their visiting scholars. It was then in a pretty run-down area adjoining the university that has since been "urbanely renewed." The famous handball court where Enrico Fermi and his colleagues first created an atomic reaction was across the street.

Joan cried all the way back to Ann Arbor. She was five-months pregnant, and the thought of having her baby in what looked to her like a ghetto instead of the idyllic college town of Ann Arbor was hard to bear. But she was a good soldier, and in September we returned to Chicago. My academic career took off like a meteor, and my last name was of no importance. I believed that I was following a path where only one's scholarly achievements and teaching ability meant something. For the next three years, this was so.

CHAPTER NINE

THE WINDY CITY
AND
ENGLISH LIFE

It was a privilege to be in a mathematics department whose faculty roster included such world-famous names as Calderon, Zygmund, Thompson, MacLane, and Kaplansky, to sit in some of their classes or seminars, or chat with them at the daily departmental afternoon tea. I made good friends with some of the graduate students, many of whom later became outstanding scholars. My teaching load consisted of one very advanced precalculus course designed for nonscience majors, a carryover from the University of Chicago Great Books curriculum. The low teaching load for postdoctoral instructors was intended to give them time to develop their research.

I wrote my first paper while at Chicago, a small but elegant one-page note, and completed my favorite of all my publications—a slim, 160-page paperback monograph written to introduce graduate students to the modern theories of ordinary differential equations. It became sort of a classic and was in print for over thirty years. But as a research mathematician, I was to defer writing textbooks until I achieved a senior rank; the way to promotion is to publish research articles in quality journals. A process justifiably called "publish or perish."

My first task was to boil down my eighty-five-page dissertation to a twenty-page research article and get it published; after that, to begin to write papers on some related questions that arose during my research. Since some intellectual growth was expected, I began to investigate problems that were quite distinct from my dissertation research. The department provided some professional travel funds, so I was able to present papers at professional mathematics meetings. I am describing a pattern that I followed and thoroughly enjoyed for twenty-three years.

Our daughter, Christina, was born on November 10, 1963 (the Marine Corps's birthday), and to my surprise my mother, Berta, decided to fly from Mexico City to visit us and see the new baby. She had never met or seen our family, and because she had not raised me, she was unable to exercise the firm control she had over her other children—she was just my Aunt Berta. Much to Joan's relief, it was a very pleasant visit despite the December Chicago weather, and Berta even helped give Christina oatmeal soaks to relieve her diaper rash.

Our social life was similar to the one we had as graduate students. Most of our activities involved the other postdoctoral instructors and their families. Stroller trips to the nearby Museum of Science and Industry replaced the afternoon marching band practice. At an all-faculty dinner I met an Argentine postdoc who was a specialist in modern South American literature, so I got to keep up my Spanish whenever we had lunch or coffee together. There was an all-black chess club at nearby Washington Park, and I was on their interclub team. Joan and I would frequently get a group together and go to a great Mexican restaurant, El Jarocho, on the North Side. The cook was a big, no-nonsense woman from Veracruz who made fantastic seafood dishes. Only later in life was Joan able to handle spicy foods, but she could demolish a plateful of refried beans and tortillas.

In the early spring of my second year, 1965, I had to start thinking about a permanent tenure-track position. My good fortune was that Professor Magnus Hestenes of the University of California, Los Angeles (UCLA), who was an authority on variational theory and had been a professor at Chicago, had heard of my work. I was invited to Los Angeles to give a talk and shortly afterward was offered a tenure-track assistant professorship at UCLA, which has always been among the top twenty U.S. mathematics departments. I was ready to accept, but suddenly another offer appeared.

Professor Michael Barrat of the mathematics department of Manchester University in England was visiting that year at Chicago; he had read my little monograph and was very impressed with it. Since his department needed a faculty member knowledgeable in the modern theory of ordinary differential equations, he offered me a one-year visiting-lecturer appointment with all travel expenses paid for my family and me. We had no more than a small trunk load of adult and children's clothes, a few books, household essentials, and a little fishing tackle; it was an ideal time for us to consider an overseas trip and an opportunity hard to refuse. But what to do about the UCLA offer?

I called the chairman of the UCLA Department of Mathematics to discuss my quandary, and to my great surprise he agreed that the Manchester offer was a fine opportunity. If I accepted the UCLA offer, he would arrange for the first year to be an unpaid leave of absence so I could go to England. I was surprised and flattered, since this kind of arrangement was usually made only to lure distinguished senior scholars. Probably Professor Hestenes played some role in the negotiations with the UCLA academic administration. I said yes to UCLA, and we were off to the British Isles!

In England we rented a modest, two-story house in the village of Didsbury, a suburb of Manchester. The owner was an

American expat professor who was an authority on the works of Nathaniel Hawthorne. The house was in a cul-de-sac and had poor heating, a tiny refrigerator, and two cats. The main street of the village had a fine array of shops; there was a library and good bus connections to Manchester, as well as an excellent local pub where I would frequently stop for a pint on the way home from work. I knew I had become one of the regulars when I was asked if I played cribbage—"Hey Yank, do you play crib?" When I replied affirmatively, I became a member of the regular evening game. An even more convincing sign of my acceptance came one evening when I arrived at the pub a few minutes after closing time because the bus was late. The pub owner was finishing putting the cloth covers on the pumps, but winked and reached under the covers and poured me a pint—a definite violation of English drinking laws.

It was before the days of the British supermarket, so Joan would watch the neighbor ladies go through their daily food-purchasing ritual: grab the cloth shopping bag; maybe walk the four blocks to the main street; stop at the butcher shop (which also sold pet food), the bakery, the green grocer, and maybe a few other shops; fill the shopping bag with the day's victuals and maybe one or two cans of pet food; and then come home. Not for Joan! She purchased a three-foot tall, wheeled shopping cart, walked to the village once a week, filled the cart, and pulled it home, while simultaneously pushing the stroller with Christina in it. She became well known around the village. One day when she stopped at the butcher shop and ordered a case of cat food, the butcher asked if we were raising a Bengal tiger. It took him several days to fill the order.

I was not courageous enough to drive on the left-hand side of the road, so we never rented a car, but in those days the bus and rail services were superb. We visited London several times and went to York and Edinburgh. The bus service to the university, about three miles down the main road, was excellent, except for one unbelievably thick evening fog, when all the bus services were cancelled and traffic stopped. I had never seen such a dense fog; I walked the three miles home never being able to see more than six feet in front of me.

I taught two courses, which initially was a slightly unnerving experience. British undergraduates who are majoring in a subject solely take courses in that subject—with maybe an occasional elective—and graduate in three years. They take all their general education courses in secondary school. An American mathematics undergraduate takes approximately 40 hours of mathematics out of 120 hours over four years. So in general, the British undergraduate is better prepared. However, American graduate education is much more rigorous, so things even out.

At the time I taught in England, the only course requirements were a series of lengthy exams at the end of each year, and the totals at the end of the three years determined the student's class standing and the nature of the degree. Consequently, the students sat in class the whole term, took copious notes, and rarely asked questions, so I had little feedback on the class material or my presentation. But just before the exams were scheduled, my office was a madhouse, with students asking questions about topics on which I may have lectured three months before.

One of the real pleasures of my time in England was to renew my love of fly-fishing on the streams of nearby Derbyshire. There was the famous Peacock Inn in Rowsley on the River Wye in Derbyshire and a lovely country hotel on the Manifold River; both had fishing rights on the rivers. (All trout fishing in Great Britain is on private waters, except for some public reservoirs.) Both streams were accessible from Manchester by bus, which I took several times until I discovered that my next-door neighbor was a fisherman. Then we would go in his car.

I was once mistaken for a poacher fishing on the Manifold since I was wearing my usual blue jeans, wool shirt, gum boots, and canvas creel instead of the traditional Hardy Brothers blazer, green rubber waders, a deerslayer cap, and maybe a tie. My accuser was a wealthy Midlands industrialist who jumped out from behind a bush, threatened to call the bailiff, and dashed back to the hotel to report me. He found out my identity and made up for his gaffe with a round of drinks, a good dinner, and a tour in his Rolls Royce of the famous Derbyshire waters where the renowned angler Izaak Walton fished. My tour guide turned out to be a nice guy once you got past his status-induced stuffiness; the little country hotel and the stream were his only escape from the demands of his work.

I really fell in love with England, its history and culture, love of learning, and less frantic academic life—and the fishing helped a little, too. The department had a position as senior lecturer open and encouraged me to apply. I decided to do so and work out my apologies to UCLA if I was successful, but Joan stepped in. She asked me how often we would visit the United States so that our children could see their grandparents if I was appointed. I naively replied, "Probably every three years," and that put the kibosh on the whole deal.

I never regretted the decision to return to the United States and UCLA, but my love for the British Isles has never waned. In 1982, I spent a wonderful six months at the University of Wales, Aberystwyth, and in 1986 I had a month-long research appointment at Oxford University. We have subscribed to the *Guardian Weekly* and the *Financial Times* for years. My memories are always refreshed when I fish with the lovely, small-stream, split-bamboo rod, especially made for me by Foster Brothers of Ashbourne, Derbyshire. It never bothered me that my name was sometimes pronounced "Sanshay." The British respect academics and tolerate eccentrics, and I fit in just fine.

CHAPTER TEN

WESTWOOD DAYS

In the late summer of 1966, we flew from Manchester to Kennedy Airport. It looked like going through customs was going to be a real ordeal—our bags were filled with clothes, toys, books, and fishing tackle, mostly purchased in England. We had two tired, cranky children and were faced with a tough inspector who seemed ready to open every suitcase. When we came up, he examined the baggage tags, which gave UCLA as our address since we had no residence.

"UCLA! Is that where you're going?"

"Yes sir, I have a teaching job there."

"Well, you know that's where John Wooden coaches—he's the greatest. You're going to see some fabulous basketball."

All the time he was okaying every one of our bags with his marker and never opened one.

We stayed at one of the airport hotels in order to get ready for the cross-country leg. We ordered hamburgers and cokes for the children, Joan collapsed, and I went down to the bar to have a year-long awaited date with an ice-cold bottle of American beer. On the first swallow, my throat locked up and I choked. I had to explain to the bartender who rushed over that I had spent a year drinking room-temperature British pints. Two swallows later, I was okay.

Upon arriving in Los Angeles, we moved into a classic 1930s California beach house on Fourth Street in Santa Monica (hence, four blocks from the beach). Later we moved to a newly constructed three-bedroom apartment with carport on Fifth Street, our home for the next eleven years. The campus was in Westwood, about thirty minutes away using the outstanding Santa Monica bus system, which ran frequently, early and late.

An annual parking permit for the UCLA staff and faculty parking lots cost one hundred dollars or more, depending on how many flights of stairs you wanted to descend, and I never purchased one. If most major companies can furnish free parking for their employees, why shouldn't universities? Probably I was the only faculty member of sixty in the mathematics department who didn't drive to work, and I knew at least six who lived close to the bus line. The bus line saved me from freeway gluts and gridlocks, and since Santa Monica was at the start of the line, I could always get a seat. I looked forward every morning to my thirty minutes to spruce up a lecture, read a novel or technical paper, or just daydream.

I was assigned a shared office in a four-office complex, with the other offices occupied by the other assistant professors, and was given a two-course teaching load. My UCLA career began with the familiar work schedule—teaching, doing research, and attending seminars, colloquia and faculty meetings—but with the added heavy pressure of obtaining tenure, which came with promotion to associate professor. This meant publishing high-quality papers in recognized journals, maybe writing a book on a research topic—but not a textbook—and receiving strong letters of recommendation on my work from experts in my field. Salt this with a little service on some university committee and achieving satisfactory (sometimes barely) teaching scores.

The tenure outcome depended on a vote of the associate and full professors, usually four to six years from the date of initial appointment. There was no more tragic experience for me than to know close colleagues who didn't make it and were informed their appointment would be terminated. This happened after the following year, so they would have time to find another faculty position. From the day they received the notification to the day they left, many were like automatons, solely coming to campus to teach class, then going home.

When I arrived at UCLA in 1966, the protest era was in full swing: marches and demonstrations against the Vietnam War, fiery speeches by Angela Davis on black power, protests by César Chávez and the United Farm Workers, the Black Panthers, and early supporters of the women's liberation movement. The very liberal faculty in the department would buttonhole me in the hallways to sign a petition, which I usually did, or ask me to join a demonstration, which I usually didn't. *National Review* and the *Guardian Weekly* were on my nightstand; I religiously watched William Buckley's *Firing Line*, and greatly admired Adlai Stevenson and Teddy Roosevelt—so what was I? To me it didn't matter—I was a mathematician, father and husband, and fisherman.

One day a campus-wide protest march took place, and I stepped out into the hallway to watch the crowds of students march through the building. I was amused to see a towering, seven-foot redhead yelling and waving a placard in the midst of what comparatively looked like midgets. It was the basketball star Bill Walton, in his radical days.

In 1968, I got pushed into the center arena by Luis Ortiz, a Mexican American student from East Los Angeles and one of our mathematics majors. He made an appointment with me to discuss the Chicano/Mexican American student situation at UCLA. The university then had an enrollment of about twenty-eight thousand in a city of nearly three million with a huge Mexican American population, largely residing in East Los Angeles. But there were less than a hundred Mexican American undergraduate students enrolled at the university. There were only three Mexican American faculty members in the tenure-track ranks. The situation was no better at the other five University of California campuses.

The East Los Angeles high school students were organizing large-scale walkouts at the three major high schools to protest the high dropout rates and the poor quality of their education. The UCLA Mexican American students had formed an organization, UMAS—United Mexican American Students—, dedicated to supporting the walkouts, and its goals included improving the situation at UCLA. Other chapters of UMAS were springing up on campuses in the Southwest, all dedicated to improving the education of Mexican American students. Luis asked me to be the faculty advisor of UMAS at UCLA, and I accepted.

Did I become radicalized? Grow a beard and ponytail? Wear a brown beret festooned with Viva Zapata buttons? No, but I did give several fiery speeches at East Los Angeles community meetings (the long-dormant thespian returns), help organize large protest marches (the Marine Corps training returns) at the Los Angeles School Board, and participate in meetings and sit-ins with the UMAS students at the administrative offices of UCLA. Why did I do this?

My name was right and the issue was right. I remembered my own central city high school and all the successful Mexican American graduates; the East Los Angeles students were getting a very raw deal. The UMAS students would need faculty support to obtain their goals, and a mathematician, ideologically untainted, from one of the prestigious campus departments, would be as good a start as they could get until more Mexican American faculty could be recruited. Finally, I strongly believed I could help solve what I regarded as a serious problem.

I spent fifteen to twenty hours a week serving on a large community group that was pushing for improvements in the East Los Angeles schools and chaired by the passionate Reverend Vahac Mardirosian. My colleagues included Sal Castro, the inspirational high school teacher who played a major role in the walkouts; Oscar Zeta Acosta (the "Brown Buffalo"), the sidekick of Hunter Thompson and activist lawyer who freed many a protester from jail; the Brown Berets, whose leader was a big, tall kid also named David Sanchez; and Joe Barry, a brilliant Harvard-trained, Mexican American linguist and bilingual teacher on the UCLA staff. He was a true friend and helped me keep my sanity. Together we spent many late hours on the freeways going back and forth to lengthy meetings (as all Mexican American meetings tend to be).

There were some perils in these activities. The Los Angeles Sheriff's Department hated protesters and was not liked by the Mexican American and black communities. Arrests were frequent, and we all knew we were being watched. Joan, my wife, will never forget one afternoon when she would normally have been away but was home sick. She heard the front door handle rattling, peeked out the window, and saw a man in a suit trying to get in the apartment. She ran to the phone in the back bedroom, and he must have heard her, because he bolted down the stairs. From a back window she saw him speed away in an unmarked car. Acosta assured us it was either a sheriff's deputy or the FBI.

On campus the major activities were pushing for more programs for recruitment of Mexican American faculty and students to UCLA and creating special courses to better prepare those students for undergraduate study. This was before any affirmative-action guidelines, so we had to rely on goodwill and community pressure; fifty or so undergraduates, a handful of graduate students, and an assistant professor of mathematics named Sánchez could hardly be called a significant lobbying force. But East Los Angeles was in ferment, and because of Joe Barry's and my strong relations with community groups demanding change, we had far more clout than our numbers would suggest. The support given by Charles Young, soon-to-be chancellor, Vice Chancellor David Saxon, and especially Assistant Vice Chancellor Elwyn Svenson was essential; they recognized the potential of the prospective Mexican American students.

In fact, the first program to recruit fifty students from East Los Angeles on full scholarships was called the High Potential Program. Its creation, interestingly enough, was due to a very insensitive act by one of the UCLA men's fraternities, Phi Kappa Psi. One weekend in the spring of 1968, they decided to have what they called a "Viva Zapata party," and hung on their front door a huge Mexican flag with the eagle in the center removed and replaced by a raised middle finger. There were "No Dogs—No Blacks—No Mexicans" signs on the building—unbelievably stupid! On Monday morning, a delegation of UMAS students, Joe Barry, and I marched into the chancellor's office and held a sit-in, demanding that the fraternity be booted off the campus.

Meanwhile, we had mobilized the community, and hundreds of phone calls of protest were flooding the administration switchboard. The Mexican Consulate heard about the incident and called. Ruben Salazar, the brilliant reporter for the *Los Angeles Times*, who was later tragically killed by the police when they fired into a bar during an East Los Angeles antiwar rally, showed up to write up the incident. We decided to use this opportunity to demand even more: the establishment of the High Potential Program and the creation of a Chicano Studies Center.

The chancellor waffled but conceded when we suggested that we would stage a demonstration the next week at the forthcoming installation of the new University of California president, Charles Hitch. The fraternity was not closed down, but all of its campus privileges, such as being able to recruit, were taken away. It was a great victory; we could give partial thanks to the Greek fraternity system.

In 1969, I was due to be considered for tenure and promotion. I needed time and peace to be able to prepare my case and wanted to get out of the department while it was being debated. Fortunately, one of the senior professors of the Division of Applied Mathematics at Brown University, Jack Hale, who was also a student of Professor Cesari, had visited at UCLA and invited me to spend the academic year at Brown. At last, after seventeen years, I finally got to go to the East! I accepted and our family was off to Providence, Rhode Island.

I enjoyed my stay in Yankee Land and at Brown, did some good research and teaching, and was glad for the break from East Los Angeles and UCLA problems. We rented a nice little house on the near-North Side, which had good bus service to the university. We discovered some excellent family-style seafood and Italian restaurants and were able to visit my Marine Corps bunkmate Sal and his family in Boston several times. For a westerner it was awesome to see big, beautiful, well-constructed houses that were built in the 1700s, when California was occupied by some scattered Native American tribes and a few Spanish friars trying to save them.

My only complaint was the quality of the public schools, which were falling apart due to lack of support and the elite appeal of private schools. Only one other member of the mathematics department sent his children to public schools. At cocktail parties the educational portfolios of our children and what private college they were going to attend was always a topic of conversation. One time, after I'd had a few drinks, a professor got me aside to tell me how much he supported the table-grape boycott by the United Farm Workers. I lit into him and called him a typical eastern liberal, willing to support some cause three thousand miles away, while letting his local schools go to hell. It was hard to explain to my son Bruce why his school desk was so ratty and the broken windows of his classroom were never repaired.

I returned to UCLA in 1970 as a tenured associate professor (hooray!) and found that the UMAS organization had grown; in my new status, I could be even more help to them. Some of my favorite UMAS students included Luis Ortiz, who recruited me and on whose mathematics education doctoral dissertation committee at Stanford I served; Juan Gomez Quiñones, a radical graduate student who became a professor of history at UCLA; Richard Tapia, one of my graduate students, who became distinguished professor of mathematics at Rice University; and Moctezuma Esparza, a leader of the high-school walkouts who became an outstanding movie producer with such films as *The Milagro Beanfield War* and *Walkout* in his credits. He and I share a laugh about his mathematics training: when he was in jail for participating in a protest march at the cathedral and needed three credit hours to graduate, I enrolled him in an introductory summer school mathematics course, entering a C on the grade sheet.

My role in the movement now was to be a facilitator and to lend credibility. At the community meetings and demonstrations, I was regarded as the UCLA representative, sans portfolio—*el Profesor Sánchez, el matematico*. On campus I was the advisor and friend of the UMAS students and quickly learned which administrative barriers needed to be breached so they could accomplish their goals. Vice Chancellor Saxon had a lot of confidence in me, maybe because he was a physicist. I regarded the Mexican American enrollment situation at UCLA and the related terrible quality of the East Los Angeles schools as catastrophic problems demanding a solution free of any ideological constraints or interpretations. This did not endear me to the growing number of Mexican American social scientists, liberals, radicals, and even a few Marxists; one historian sneeringly referred to me as "Nuts and Bolts" Sánchez, which pleased me to no end. The Chicano Movement was in full swing. At two big meetings in Denver and Santa Barbara, the student groups were encouraged to move from being solely campus oriented to working in the community under the banner of cultural nationalism. The cry was to resist the occupation by the brutal gringos of "Aztlan," the mythical birthplace of the Aztecs, which for practical purposes was that portion of the Southwest taken from Mexico by the Treaty of Guadalupe Hidalgo in 1848. The ideologists were in full control, and many of the UMAS chapters adopted the name *MEChA, Movimiento Estudiantil Chicano de Aztlan.* The speeches and the rhetoric were more fiery than before and sometimes a little wacky ("Did the gringos really steal our enchilada?"), but as long as the educational goals were there, I stuck with it.

Early in the game, I began to see that the four or five weekly drives to East Los Angeles to attend often protracted meetings, plus my on-campus activities supporting UMAS and pushing for the recruitment of more Mexican American faculty, could seriously affect my academic progress. As time went on, I saw casualties among junior faculty as a result of their involvement. To counter this I developed my Island Philosophy: I lived on three islands—Mexican American/Chicano, Mathematics, and Family—and if anybody or anything attempted to build a bridge between the islands, I would chop it down. For instance, in the mathematics department I never discussed or asked for support of my outside activities; conversations were solely about theorems, proofs, classes, and baseball, and I did a very responsible job of teaching. With my family I was the typical faculty parent and spouse and tried to make up for my frequent absences. I intended that the name Sánchez would only have significance on the first island. It worked: In 1976, I was appointed full professor of mathematics.

In 1973, I earned a one-year sabbatical leave, and I decided to spend it at the University of Wisconsin–Madison, at the Mathematics Research Institute. Madison is a very liberal college town and the state capital, situated in the middle of the cornfields. Our children found it very exciting because of the opportunities to throw snowballs and toboggan. I liked it because there was a lovely meadow trout stream about thirty minutes from the house we rented. At Wisconsin I developed a very close collaboration with Professor Fred Brauer doing research on mathematical models on the effects of harvesting (think of fishing, hunting, disease) on populations. We have written several landmark papers on the topic.

I was honored to participate in a memorable event in 1973. At a meeting of one Native American and about twenty Mexican American scientists and mathematicians in Albuquerque, an organization dedicated to increasing the number of Mexican and Native American students and faculty in the sciences was formed. The numbers were very small, largely in the life sciences; at the time we could count no more than eleven PhD mathematicians in the entire country. We named the organization SACNAS—the Society for the Advancement of Chicano and Native American Scientists. It has been a phenomenal success, now numbering over fourteen hundred students and six hundred faculty and professionals. The annual meetings are five-day events that include career counseling and scientific seminars and invited speakers of national and international distinction and culminate with a grand pow-wow. SACNAS is certainly the country's top minority science organization.

The first signal of what might be in my academic future came as I was leaving Wisconsin to return to UCLA. I received a call from Vice Chancellor Saxon asking me to serve as temporary director of the newly created UCLA Chicano Studies Center. The present director had been pressured to resign by a coalition of students and community activists, and Saxon wanted me to take the job as a half-time appointment until the search for a new director was completed. This showed a lot of confidence in me, but I told him that it was a crazy idea and strongly argued that the position required someone in the humanities or social sciences, certainly not a mathematician. But he insisted, and out of loyalty to him, I agreed. My remuneration was an extra week tacked on to my return date to UCLA so I could do some fishing in Montana.

In their early days, and sometimes even today, ethnic studies centers—black, Chicano, or other—have been a problem for many of the universities who created them, usually because of student and community pressure. The faculty and administration regarded them as research centers, conducting studies, organizing conferences, hosting visiting scholars, soliciting and being awarded grants, and publishing monographs or journals. But the activist community and students often regarded them as forums for their ideologies and programs, sometimes urging that nonacademic publications be produced and that governance be by some community-based steering committee. This could cause real troubles for the university, since insisting on more traditional standards could bring on protest demonstrations and accusations of racism. The problem of funding could also become a real problem, since, aside from an administrative operating budget, centers were, and are, expected to develop their own external support or face closure.

The scenario described above was what I stepped into when I arrived back at UCLA. A group of community activists and students, some of whom put Karl Marx and Emiliano

Zapata arm in arm on the same pedestal, were insisting on creating a steering committee and dismantling the faculty committee that was required of every center. The question of what is Chicano research and literature was the source of many heated arguments, and some newly recruited and very talented Chicano faculty stayed clear of the center. No efforts were being made to obtain outside funding; the university was expected to foot the bill for whatever projects were suggested by the proposed steering committee.

After six months, with the help of the administration and some dedicated faculty and students, and after lots of meetings, some semblance of normalcy was achieved. I was occasionally called a *vendido* (sellout) by some of the radicals, but Professor Nuts and Bolts kept pushing the notion of quality—quality of programs and research, measured by external reviews wherever possible, and quality of recruited faculty—and getting faculty to creatively think about funding for their projects. An acceptable steering committee was formed, but proprietary and research issues revolving about the center's journal, *Aztlan*, were not settled. I left them to the humanities and social sciences faculty and gratefully returned to the mathematics department.

The nine years I had spent working with students, community, and junior faculty on Mexican American educational issues were very rewarding, but the discussions and battles over affirmative-action issues were increasing. I realized that the name Sánchez would appear on more and more agendas; John Garcia, the eminent psychologist, and I were the only two Mexican American full professors at UCLA in 1976. Committees dealing with minority studies and admissions required often time-consuming minority faculty participation. They asked newly recruited Mexican American junior faculty to serve; community and student pressures, and their own dedication, made it difficult to refuse. They were told that research, teaching, and university service were the three pillars on which their promotions would be based.

What they may not have been told is that at a research university, service counts very little toward promotion of a junior faculty to tenure. Scholarly papers or books, invited research presentations at professional meetings, outside research support through grants, graduate student mentoring, and satisfactory classroom teaching are the elements of success. Nominal service on some departmental committee is usually sufficient. Not knowing that, across the country junior faculty with names like mine were recruited, and then later denied promotion. They often ended up at a lesser institution or left the academic world. While some were not academically qualified and were filling some unstated quota, many were not counseled about realities and were sold a bill of goods.

I tried to mentor the junior faculty and to relieve them of their service role where I could, but I could see that my career was becoming more and more involved with politics and moving away from mathematics and the intellectual life. Despite living in a Santa Monica apartment five blocks from the beach, Southern California was losing its attraction—maybe this is why we never bought a house. I wanted to be nearer to mountains and trout streams, wanted to continue my mathematics research, wanted to devote my remaining energy to help increase the number of Mexican American students pursuing careers in mathematics, science, and engineering, and wanted to be someplace where my name was just another entry in the faculty roster. My friends, Professor Richard Griego, chairman of the University of New Mexico Department of Mathematics and Statistics, and Professor Tom Kyner, who had moved to New Mexico from the University of Southern California, arranged an appointment for me, and in 1977 I returned to Albuquerque and my alma mater as a full professor of mathematics.

■ *Padre Cecilio, Madre Cons, and David at Balboa Park. Photo courtesy of the author.*

■ *The first catch. Photo courtesy of the author.*

A school assembly skit with Bob Shoemake. Photo courtesy of the author.

■ *San Diego High School in its glory days. Photo courtesy of the author.*

Summer training—a lighter moment. Photo courtesy of the author.

Marine Corps schools pistol team—I'm second from the right. Photo courtesy of the author.

■ *Joan and I leaving the church on a rocket launcher.*
  Photo courtesy of the author.

■ *My first teaching assignment—the University of Chicago.*
Photo courtesy of the author.

Escaping Southern California—the family in the Sequoias. Photo courtesy of the author.

The first New Mexico Christmas. Photo courtesy of the author.

■ *Lecture at the Argentine Stock Exchange, Buenos Aires. Photo courtesy of the author.*

■ *Lehigh president Peter Likins and the provost. Photo courtesy of the author.*

■ *The provost in his lair. Photo courtesy of the author.*

■ *Captain Billy Knowles and a nice bonefish. Photo courtesy of the author.*

■ *At the tenth anniversary of the Very Large Array, Magdalena, New Mexico. Photo courtesy of the author.*

CHAPTER ELEVEN

NEW MEXICO
VISIT TWO

My experience at the University of New Mexico for nine years was that of a typical senior professor: teaching, doing research, and serving on university and national committees. I was honored to have served during that time on both the Board of Governors of the Mathematical Association of America and the Council of the American Mathematical Society; I also participated on various committees for these two organizations, as well as advisory- and fellowship-selection committees for the National Science Foundation. My research went well, and I coauthored, with Professor Micha Gisser of the economics department, a paper on competition versus optimal control in ground-water pumping, which attained landmark status in resource modeling. I found a fishing partner, Lou Mogk, who was also an excellent duplicate bridge partner, a real plus.

When we moved to New Mexico, the family insisted that we buy a house, our first in nineteen years of marriage. My teenager, Christina, insisted that it had to include a dog, so we acquired and I trained an obedience-trial prize-winning Shetland sheepdog. (The family figured that I was just reliving my Marine Corps days.) The house was located in the pleasant Altura Park neighborhood, about two and a half miles by foot or bus from campus—no paid parking permits, remember?

There were fourteen David Sanchez listings in the Albuquerque phone book (now there are thirty-two), as one of my UCLA colleagues found out when he called the information operator to ask for my number. He informed her that he knew my middle initial was A, and she told him that now he was down to eight. The mixture of the three cultures, Hispanic, Native American, and Anglo was a fascinating one, but there was prejudice. My neighbor, a Hispanic businessman, once pointed out some workers remodeling a nearby house and referred to them as *surumatos*. I found out it is a pejorative slang term applied by New Mexicans to Mexican laborers, as is the term *mojados* (wetbacks).

The Spanish, Hispanic, Mexican distinctions and names were sometimes disturbing to me and often ambiguous. I would never admit to being Spanish; the term Chicano was okay, but Padre Cecilio and Madre Cons and a lot of traditionalists would have objected to it. Mexican American was fine with me, Latino was ambiguous in terms of the country, and Hispanic was a little too intellectual for me. There was amusing ambivalence, too. New Mexicans celebrate September 16, but it commemorates Mexico's winning independence from Spain in 1821. The *Virgen de Guadalupe*, much revered in New Mexico, is a Mexican icon, and the music at posh Hispanic events in Santa Fe is often played by mariachis, Mexican musical groups usually dressed in Mexican charro outfits.

So I kept my Mexicanness to myself, did good research and teaching, and worked on several programs introducing minority undergraduates to some of the problems in the interplay between mathematics and biology. Professors Griego, Henry Harpending of the anthropology department, and I got funding to support the programs. In supervising several students, I discovered that, at that time, it was very difficult to convince Hispanic undergraduates to go outside the state for graduate studies—they were very provincial.

For example, one of our research students was a very bright young lady, Mary Sanchez, a biology major with near-perfect grades. We arranged and paid for a trip for her to UCLA, where she spent several days with Professor Elma Gonzalez of the biology department being recruited for their graduate program. She turned them down and took a job at one of the labs at UNM Hospital—I was crestfallen.

But rewards can come later in life and in strange ways. Ten years later I was reading a copy of the magazine *Science* and found an article on careers for women in science. The article featured an interview with Associate Professor of Biology Mary Sanchez of Washington State University. I gave myself a long-delayed pat on the back.

In 1980, I was honored to be one of three invited speakers to lecture at *ELAM, Escuela Latino Americana de Matematicas*, a biannual, monthlong meeting of Latin American mathematics professors and graduate students, held in Mar de Plata, Argentina. While there, I was asked to go to Buenos Aires to give a lecture to the distinguished board of directors of the Argentine Stock Exchange. I lectured on population modeling, and in the course of the talk, I mentioned that while Argentines were big beef eaters, they had an excellent cold-water fishery off the Falkland Islands. An icy chill went across the room, and an admiral in the front row politely informed me that in Argentina, they were called the *Islas Malvinas!* I made the same mistake again, and this time the correction was not so polite. The next year the Falkland Islands War between Great Britain and Argentina took place; some of my British friends accused me of starting it.

In 1982, I took a one-semester sabbatical leave to the University College of Wales, Aberystwyth, which I selected because one of its faculty members, Professor Noel Lloyd, was a real expert in one of my fields of research and because Wales had good trout fishing. The town of Aberystwyth sits on the Irish

Sea in mid-Wales; the surrounding area is a stunning combination of mountains and ocean. My landlord was a minister, so on Sundays I would accompany him and his family to a Welsh Methodist Church. Since the hymns were the same ones I sang as a boy, except they were in Welsh, I faked the words and sang along. When Joan visited me for the last two weeks of my leave, one of the ladies of the church told her that she should be proud of the way I had mastered the hymns. Nobody ever asked about my name.

North Wales is the heart of Welsh nationalism, but mid-Wales is not far behind, as I discovered one day when my landlady's brother took me fishing. It was the usual wet, spring day, and we decided to stop in a country pub for a beer and a sandwich. When we walked in, he went over to chat briefly with some friends, and I walked over to the bar and ordered a pint of bitter. The bartender scowled at me, moved to the other end of the bar, and started washing glasses. I ordered again, a little louder. It looked like this was going to have no effect, when my fishing companion walked over and in a loud voice proclaimed, "Everybody, this is my friend David. He's an American!" There were cheers, slaps on the back, and the beer flowed. It was obvious that because of my accent, they had assumed that I was a despised Englishman.

I left Wales with the same feelings I had when I left Manchester sixteen years earlier—wishing I could stay. Great Britain holds an attraction for me, a fit with my intellectual and personal traits, and a love of their people that I cannot explain but am grateful for.

Whatever leadership skills I had acquired as a Marine Corps lieutenant must have surfaced when I was in New Mexico, because I was appointed chair of the Department of Mathematics and Statistics and later was elected president of the University of New Mexico Faculty Senate. Possibly my only notable accomplishment was leading a protest and vote of no confidence against the board of regents in 1986. There is a picture of me in the *Chronicle of Higher Education* at the podium melodramatically rallying the seven hundred faculty members present to Shakespeare's "Cry 'Havoc' and let slips the dogs of war!" What a hamburger I was—this produced cheers and passionate applause, but as expected, only resulted in more rounds of inconclusive meetings with the governor and the president of the board of regents, who was a former governor and UNM football star.

In the spring of 2009, a similar vote of no confidence occurred at the University. I believe these votes reflect a failure of the regental appointment process. Regents in New Mexico and many other states are appointed by the governor, and if he chooses political cronies or people with an axe to grind (e.g., eliminating tenure), or people, usually alumni, convinced they know more about education than the deans and faculty, then there will be problems. Professional organizations offer workshops and issue educational publications designed to guide university boards of governance. Regents should take advantage of them. In some states regents are elected by popular vote—good idea? The verdict is out.

In 1986, a dramatic turn in my life plan, if I had one, came when I received a call from Professor Everett Pitcher, secretary of the American Mathematical Society, informing me that he had nominated me as a candidate for the position of provost and vice president of Lehigh University. This fit a pattern I later recognized—of all the jobs I held as faculty or administrator, I was nominated or appointed and never applied for them. For mathematics positions, the selections were based on my research accomplishments and had nothing to do with the name Sánchez, but now I began to wonder.

Pitcher was familiar with my mathematical accomplishments. He had witnessed or was aware of my service on several professional and governmental committees. I was not unhappy with New Mexico, but the thought of being a provost was interesting, so I decided to accept the nomination. The decision was more attractive when I found out that the president of Lehigh was Peter Likins, whom I had known as an outstanding engineering professor at UCLA; I had served on several of his doctoral committees. He later became president of the University of Arizona.

There were twenty candidates, some of whom were probably deans and had far more administrative experience than I, with a three-year term as chair of a department of thirty-five faculty with a modest budget (about $1 million). I told Joan that I had a 5 percent chance and that she didn't need to call the movers. Then the pool shrank to ten, so I had a 10 percent chance. I visited the campus for a screening interview and survived; the pool shrank to five; I told Joan we should get a little serious, maybe get some change of address cards. My spare time was spent doing a real in-depth analysis of the academic programs, administrative structure, and budget of the university. I saw that there were terrific challenges in trying to transform a long established, and probably quite conservative, engineering school. The pool shrank to three—now I had a strenuous visit, meeting with the search committee, administrators, faculty, and students. One of the more serious students interviewing me was the son of a lieutenant in the 12th Marines. I broke him up when I told him I had drunk a lot of Ten-Cents Pabst with his old man. Paul Franz, the vice president for development, and an absolute genius at convincing donors to give big dollars, was on the search committee. He was very pleased that I fished and played bridge.

In June 1986, Likins flew to Albuquerque to offer me the job, and so I was off to Bethlehem, Pennsylvania.

CHAPTER TWELVE

PAPER-PUSHING DAYS
PRIVATE AND FEDERAL

It was a great job. Likins was trying to move the university from a school primarily recognized for its engineering programs and intercollegiate wrestling prowess to a more comprehensive institution. As academic boss, I had major responsibilities, along with my four excellent deans, to help accomplish that. The school had only recently admitted women students, but powerful alumni pressure, with threats to drop financial support, resisted some of the changes. The changes eventually came to pass: the school's nickname is no longer the Engineers but the Mountain Hawks, commemorating a 600-foot-high hill behind the campus, whimsically (to me) named South Mountain.

I worked a lot with the deans and department chairs, but also participated in the frequent meetings of the board of trustees, who were a much different cut than the University of New Mexico Board of Regents. At Lehigh they were mostly self-made men, not political aspirants or scions of blue-blood families but men who had made their fortunes in business or finance. They were a no-nonsense bunch who got down to business and wrapped it up. Whatever disagreements they had were settled in closed sessions. Almost all of them were very loyal Lehigh University engineering alumni. In the years I was provost, I witnessed the development of a magnificent arts-and-performance center that served the whole Lehigh Valley, a new football stadium and athletic fields, and a huge engineering laboratory complex on South Mountain. All this came about through the efforts and contributions of the board and the work of Paul Franz.

In a way, administration is much easier in a private university, because there are no state bureaucracies to deal with, but this is counterbalanced by the cold reality that about 60 percent of the operating expenses have to be financed through student tuition. The percentage is much less at state universities. Lehigh is in competition for students with many of the private colleges and technical universities in the East (there seem to be hundreds of them), and because of limits on classroom and dormitory space, a cap has to be put on the size of the first-year class. But expenses, which are rising, have to be met. This means increasing tuition but keeping it comparable to that reported by competitors. It's a very tough game.

The budget meetings, which began in the early fall, were long and involved, but not acrimonious. They were chaired by the president, with each of the deans present and fighting for their college's share. My job was to coordinate and referee their requests, rewarding excellence and innovation wherever possible. Finally, the grand denouement came in the spring, when the next year's class size numbers were in. We either made our budget or would have to make sometimes painful adjustments. The budgetary exercise was great experience and proved invaluable to me in some of my later administrative jobs.

Lehigh University is in South Bethlehem, once filled with steel mills and the headquarters of the now-defunct giant, Bethlehem Steel. It was an ethnic melting pot because of the presence of the steelworkers and their families. The middle and upper classes mostly lived across the Lehigh River in Moravian-founded, historical North Bethlehem or in country homes in the surrounding Lehigh Valley. The valley contains the towns of Bethlehem, Allentown, and Easton, home of historic rival, Lafayette College, and there are three other private colleges within a thirty-mile radius. The Lehigh-Lafayette football rivalry is the most played in the nation: the two teams have met 145 times since 1884. There was no Sanchez in the Bethlehem phone book; Ricardo Viera, a wild Cuban and the Lehigh University Museum curator, provided my only opportunity to speak Spanish, and there was a tiny Mexican restaurant in downtown Bethlehem to meet my needs for an occasional enchilada.

One of the valuable qualifications that I had as a provost was that I had been a faculty member for twenty-three years and a department chair for three. Consequently, I knew the turf on both sides of the fence and could understand passionate—and sometimes a little unrealistic—faculty or departmental requests. The long tradition of engineers serving as provost was broken by my appointment, and I think that helped as we moved to become more than a technical university.

I remember an incident that serves as a good example. One afternoon the chair of the music department, a tempestuous, Harvard-trained Italian American, barged into my office and joyously announced that his department had just received a $6,000 grant from the National Endowment for the Arts to support a concert series. Lehigh was accustomed to receiving huge grants to support engineering projects, so this amount wouldn't even classify as peanuts. But I knew what the award meant to the arts program, so I grabbed the man, and we dashed across the hall into the president's office and exuberantly announced the award.

Living in Pennsylvania had its advantages for me. It was a state acclaimed for its trout fishing, although opening day on most of its streams looked like a political convention. This was my first experience with private fishing and hunting clubs, many of which were founded long ago by wealthy capitalists for the benefits of their families and friends. I visited one club that had its own brook-trout hatchery and warming sheds with grills at locations next to the stream. Club members could arrange for one of the club employees to bring wine and garnishes and barbecue the trout on the spot.

One day a very senior, retired chairman of Bethlehem Steel invited Paul Franz and me to join him for a day at his exclusive fishing club. He picked us up in his chauffeured limousine and on the way to the stream turned to me and asked in a very loud voice (he was quite deaf from all his years on the mill floor), "Dave, do you know why I took up fishing?"

"No sir, I don't."

"It's because all of those golf guys—THEY'RE ALL DEAD!"

While at Lehigh, I realized that the Florida Keys and their great fishing were much closer than my beloved Western streams. I could take a three-hour flight to Miami, rent a car, and then be in Islamorada two hours later. There I could stalk the elusive bonefish, the "grey ghost of the flats," a spooky five to fifteen pound fish that when hooked will burn off a hundred yards of line in a split second. Bonefishing fulfilled a dream of mine that started in my youth, when I read every fishing book in the San Diego Public Library. With the help of a great guide, Captain Billy Knowles, I have been fishing the flats since 1987.

Fishing, especially fly fishing, has always played a great curative role in my life. The water, the surroundings, the stalking of the prey, the magnificent mental shot when the initial strike occurs, even a fishless day trying to unlock the secret of why the fish are not biting—all make it easy to completely forget mathematical problems or administrative crises. At the end of the day, when asked "Did you catch anything?" the possible answer "No, but I had a great day" is an easy one.

Another real benefit of being at Lehigh was that Bethlehem was an hour bus ride to the Port Authority Bus Terminal in the heart of Manhattan. This provided Joan and me with museum visits, performances at the Metropolitan Opera—a lifelong dream fulfilled—and shopping, with Zabar's Deli and kitchen-gadget shop, my favorite, and Bloomingdale's, Joan's favorite. Regretfully, I never got to the Bronx Zoo, whose curator and herpetologist, Raymond Ditmars, was my boyhood idol. But after a day, or at most two, in New York City, the crowds and aggressiveness would get to me, and I had to get back to the serenity of the Lehigh Valley.

For me, the only drawback in my university administrative career was the minimal contact with the lifeblood of any school, the students. I loved teaching and the classroom and campus interactions, but the students later became just numbers on a budget page, and I missed them. One day when I was walking up to the provost's office, my secretary came running out the door and exclaimed, "Dr. Sánchez, there are thirty students sitting in your office. Shall I call the university police?"

The students were protesting moving a chemistry lab to a more remote location. Sit-ins were old stuff to me from my UCLA days, and I replied, "Absolutely not! Just order some cookies and soft drinks." Then I went into my office, sat on the floor, and started negotiating.

I think I accomplished quite a bit at Lehigh; my administrative skills were greatly sharpened. Largely from watching the board of trustees, I learned how to chair a meeting getting to the main issues and politely squeezing down the needless rhetoric that is a characteristic of almost any meeting with faculty. Every eminence usually has to express his or her learned judgment, whether it is relevant or not. The humanities and social sciences, besieged by engineers, finally had a champion in the provost's office. It took me three years, working patiently with faculty committees, to get the tenure-and-promotion policy in line with that of quality universities, but I was never able to solve the applied mathematics problem. The mathematics department was strongly opposed to tarnishing its course offerings with any mathematics that might prove useful in analyzing real-world phenomena. At a university like Lehigh, that made no sense whatsoever.

I missed having long stretches of time to do mathematical research, but I kept my grey cells stimulated by writing fiction, mostly short stories having something to do with fishing, but I tried a couple of mystery novels. Although I have written more than thirty research papers and authored or coauthored four mathematics books, I think it is tougher to write dialogue than a mathematical expression. Like any writer, I have a manila folder filled with rejection slips.

I had decided that I liked academic administration, had some ability in it, and the provostship was a good job. Then in 1990, dramatic turn number two occurred when Erich Bloch, distinguished director of the National Science Foundation (NSF) and retired IBM vice president, called to ask me to serve a two-year appointment as assistant director, with responsibility for the Directorate of Mathematical and Physical Sciences. The directorate supports the Astronomy, Chemistry, Materials Science, Mathematics, and Physics Divisions; it is the largest directorate in the foundation and, at the time, had a budget of nearly $600 million. Managing it is certainly one of the top jobs in federal science administration, giving the opportunity for an inside view of how scientific research and education receive government support. The NSF portfolio of research centers, astronomical observatories and telescopes, laboratories, individual researchers, and fellowship awardees is staggering. In addition, it has a huge program in science and mathematics education, supporting students, teachers, and faculty.

Accepting the appointment meant stepping down from the provostship and upon returning to Lehigh two years later, becoming a member of the mathematics department, with which I had no real bond. Some people told me that the appointment was a sure stepping stone to a university presidency—a job I never wanted because it was too far removed from the academic pulse. Joan agreed, because she knew that I do not suffer fools easily; a few meetings with testy alumni or legislators who care more about the athletic programs than the English department, and I would be turning in my nameplate.

My undergraduate major was mathematics with a philosophy minor, and except for a freshman course in astronomy and a graduate course in physical optics, which I barely passed, I took no college courses in science. Whatever chemistry I learned in high school had long since passed into the ether. But my lack of a science background was not so important, since the real job of an assistant director was to develop a budget, champion the programs of the divisions at internal planning meetings and external congressional hearings, and spend much time with external disciplinary advisory committees setting priorities. My experience as a provost looked like it would make a good fit, so I accepted the appointment.

Affirmative action and the need for diversity were moving into high gear, which meant the name Sánchez took on additional significance. My fair skin and unaccented English didn't fit stereotypes and may have convinced some that I was Latin American or Spanish. When I introduced myself, I would use the accented Spanish pronunciation of my name, which would sometimes result in raised eyebrows or a quizzical glance. But the real problem was that there was a not-uncommon belief that slots were being filled with minority individuals whose qualifications were below those of majority candidates.

Hence, for many blacks and Latinos (the currently accepted classification), there were internal pressures to show that appointments were deserved by virtue of talents and not ethnicity. Being the token minority is stressful, but the antidote—demonstrating intelligence and self-confidence—can be hard to develop and sustain. For me it was not difficult—my name was Sánchez and my vita spoke for itself. Unfortunately I couldn't carry it hung on my neck. Being a mathematician might have helped a little because of our ascribed aura of intelligence, but in a nutshell, you have to show that "you're smarter than the average bear."

Moving Joan and our household goods to Washington, D.C., for a two-year period made no sense, so she stayed in our house in Bethlehem. I rented an apartment in Baltimore, four blocks from the train station, which had very good commuter train service to downtown Washington, D.C. (The apartment was a three-hour weekend drive to Bethlehem.) On the train I met Dr. Norine Noonan, a senior budget officer for the Office of Management and Budget, which oversees the entire federal budget. Our conversations put me on a steep learning curve on how science was funded. I was so impressed with her intelligence that I tried to convince her that she was wasting her life as a D.C. drone. She is now a vice chancellor at one of the Florida state universities.

While I was assistant director, I visited some of the NSF-supported facilities, including the astronomical observatories in the Chilean Andes. I also attended many disciplinary advisory committee meetings, where an undercurrent that NSF was holding back created a lot of tensions—"You NSF dirty rats didn't give us the money we requested." There is never enough money to satisfy the insatiable academics, but I discovered that the much-maligned program officers deserved great praise. They were very responsible, knowledgeable, and hard working, trying to make a finite pot of money support the best and most promising research possible. There had to be some losers, but they picked great winners and earned my respect.

Disappointing, however, were the meetings of the science committees of the U.S. Congress and Senate. The NSF senior staff had to testify every year before the House and the Senate committees responsible for approving the budget request for the coming year. I envisioned a smaller version of what we see on TV when hearings are broadcast: the director or I seated at a table, the entire committee formidably lined up at the front of the room, seated on an elevated podium, the room filled with staff and onlookers, fiery testimony, some reporters and maybe a TV camera or two. I was very excited when we lined up outside the meeting room at the House or Senate building, but was I disappointed!

The room was usually small and dingy and could hardly fit the audience. The director or I, if my directorate was testifying, would sit at a table in front of the committee, with staff right behind us to whisper information if needed; the committee was strung out at tables directly in front. There were ten or more legislators on the committee, but usually never more than three or four listened to the testimony. They would walk in and out, with others replacing them, talk to their staff, occasionally ask a question, maybe rush off to catch another hearing, and pay desultory attention. One senior representative from California would sometimes light up his morning cigar. No TV cameras—the only reporters present were one or two from the science newsletters—and the only excitement might be when a legislator would get fired up about some demographic data. The testimony was about the distribution of billions of dollars, but a meeting of your local township's gardening and landscaping council would likely be far more stimulating.

The most notable funding incident during my two years involved a $45 million proposal for the National High Magnetic Field Laboratory. The competitors were Massachusetts Institute of Technology, which had a longstanding research history in the subject, well-developed laboratories, and trained personnel; and Florida State University, which only had some land, three very talented and dynamic senior researchers, and collaborations arranged with the University of Florida and Los Alamos National Laboratory. But the clincher for me was the commitment of funds by the University of Florida Chancellor for Higher Education and the governor of Florida for building the laboratory and creating new faculty positions. On the basis of the analysis provided to me by two of my very talented program officers and my own gut feelings about the Florida commitment, I recommended to Director Bloch that the award be given to Florida State. He agreed and the clamor began!

The president of MIT, who had had previous disputes with Bloch, was furious and wrote letters to Congress and threatened a lawsuit. The Boston newspapers vilified me, and Representative Joseph Kennedy wanted to subpoena me for a hearing. On the lighter side, my close friend Sal told me there was a contract out on me, and that I should not visit him unless I traveled at night and in disguise. But the director supported me, and the controversy over the decision eventually died down. The laboratory has been a phenomenal success.

On the wall of my study is a personally signed letter from President George H. W. Bush, dated November 16, 1990, thanking me for an invitation to fish for steelhead trout in the Northwest waters and for sending him a picture of a sizeable bonefish I had caught in Islamorada. He signed personal letters with a thick, black felt-tip pen, and there was his signature and the inscription "Loved that bonefish picture." My secretary, a real Washington pro, had said my letter would never reach the Oval Office and would get a pro forma, machine signature reply. I told her to call and mention George Hommel, the president's Florida Keys guide and a friend of mine. She later said that probably nobody in the NSF had ever gotten a personal letter from the president, to which I replied, "That's because they don't fish."

I believe my two years as assistant director were successful, and I learned a lot about the process of how the government funds scientific research. For instance, I figured out that because of the planning, budget approval process, and the hearings, it takes three years from the time a major project is proposed until the check is written. This fact must be considered in any planning strategy. The contacts I made with the permanent NSF program officers and staff were useful in my later career, and I learned some of the key elements of a successful proposal. Erich Bloch completed his six-year appointment after my first year, and if he had stayed, I would have tried to work permanently at the NSF.

When it was getting close to the time to go, I was in a quandary about my future. Nothing interesting came up, so in the summer of 1992 I returned to Lehigh and somewhat disconsolately sat in an office in the mathematics department. But then, out of the blue, Sig Hecker, the director of the Los Alamos National Laboratory, called to offer me the position of deputy associate director for research and education, based on my background, my familiarity with the Southwest, and surely my last name. This time that was not a problem for me, since my major responsibility would be to develop outreach programs in mathematics and science education to benefit New Mexican K–12 students and teachers. The majority of them in northern New Mexico were Hispanic or Native American, so my name, along with my qualifications, might open a few doors. It seemed like a great opportunity since I believed the personnel and the facilities had terrific potential to accomplish this goal. Besides, it was a chance to return to my beloved Southwest, so I accepted the offer.

It was a dismal failure. The organization of the laboratory is very cliquish and as a newcomer I was not part of the culture. I think many of the personnel believed they were working for the "University of California of the Jemez Mountains," and aside from maintaining the superiority of Los Alamos High School for their children, they had little interest in outreach to the New Mexico school population. The laboratory runs an annual high school computer competition, and the year I was there, it was won by a trio of Hispanic students from Española High School. A lot of the Los Alamos folks reacted with shocked disbelief. Los Alamos County has one of the country's highest per capita incomes and is close to 100 percent Anglo and Republican. This does not endear it to the poorer neighboring Hispanic and Native American communities from which it draws many of its lower-paid workers.

Most of the divisions of the laboratory were jealously guarded fiefdoms, looking out for their own interests, and the Department of Energy supported this organizational Balkanization. Senior Washington energy officials acted like Tammany Hall bosses dispensing handouts. I discovered two more groups in the lab that were developing science-education initiatives, and neither of them would collaborate with my staff.

In 1993, pandemonium struck when Secretary of Energy Hazel O'Leary decided to reorganize the entire Los Alamos National Laboratory into a total quality management/parallel management structure. This effort was a complete disaster. Entire divisions were dismantled, eminent senior scientists lost their status and many resigned, and junior staff were demoted and had to go through a search process to reapply for a position. Being a new arrival with no seniority and minimal membership in the lab culture, I was one of the casualties. I was faced with trying to find an equivalent slot or being demoted.

It was a demeaning experience. Hecker was sincerely apologetic, but his hands were tied.

In looking back, there is nothing positive I can say about my Los Alamos experience, except that Joan and I have maintained a close friendship with one of my staff, Dr. Fred Begay, a Navajo PhD physicist, and his wife, Helen. They even took Joan on a wild trip to Shiprock, New Mexico, to attend a Navajo fair. The one amusing lab incident happened when I decided I wanted a top secret clearance, which usually took a year but could be greatly expedited if one was willing to take a lie detector test. Nobody at the Lab had ever tried this route, but I decided to do it. I went down to Sandia National Laboratories in Albuquerque and got wired to the machine. The test administrator, a spooky kind of guy, informed me that I had not passed the test. "There were some problems with your answers to questions about engaging in possible sabotage activities. Can we talk about it?"

"Sure. Let me think—I did see *The Guns of Navarone* movie twice, and I've read a lot of John Le Carré novels. As a boy I broke a few windows with my BB gun, and that's about it."

"Hmm—well maybe that's what causing the problems with your responses. Let's try that section again."

I passed the test and got my top secret clearance despite my saboteur tendencies.

I was feeling depressed when dramatic turn number three occurred and my name and reputation came to the rescue. I was contacted by a search committee of the Texas A&M University system and asked to apply for the position of vice chancellor for academic affairs. I had just broken my ankle sliding down a bank while fishing the Conejos River in Colorado, so carrying crutches, I flew to Houston to be interviewed by the search committee. I got a firsthand look at some of the regents I would have to deal with—there was not a liberal in the bunch. Several days later I was offered the job, and I accepted.

CHAPTER THIRTEEN

A BRIEF TEXAS INTERLUDE

The Texas A&M system consists of the monster flagship university, Texas A&M, with over forty thousand students, and six (now eight) smaller regional universities, one of which, Prairie View A&M, is a historically black university. The system also houses a large number of engineering and agricultural agencies with offices all over Texas. Each university has its own president and reports to the system, which is headed by a chancellor who reports to a board of regents appointed by the governor. It appeared to me that it provided a wonderful structure within which to improve the quality of Texas higher education, especially for its Mexican American and black population, and to develop quality programs to improve K–12 teacher education.

Then there was the problem of moving. Joan, my trooper of a wife, was getting tired of leaving places she learned to love—Westwood, Bethlehem, Los Alamos—and now was faced with moving to the humid farming land of south central Texas. It was flat, with the nearest mountains a quarter of a continent away. College Station was completely a university town called Aggieland, filled with fanatical students called Aggies, and infested with fire ants, as Joan discovered when she walked across an empty lot to examine a prospective house.

Then there was the admission that I, a native Californian and loyal New Mexican, would be living in Texas, which to some must have seemed some kind of penance. I always remembered the bumper sticker I once saw in Taos that read, "If God had wanted Texans to ski, he would have given them mountains." It was followed the next year with one that read, "If God had wanted New Mexicans to ski, he would have given them money." The anti-littering signs on the highway said "Don't Mess with Texas." I wouldn't dare.

But we had no real options, and in the fall of 1993 I accepted the offer. We sold our lovely house in Los Alamos and bought an equally lovely house in College Station, to discover that, like many Texans, all our neighbors were helpful, friendly people; we soon became very close friends. The Mexican Americans were just like the ones from my youth in San Diego; they weren't obsessed with the Spanish heritage, but I thought Tex-Mex food was best left for tourists. Texas is a huge state—if a person in El Paso wants to go to the beach, San Diego, California, is closer than Brownsville, Texas—but its highway system is superb. Nearby Houston has an outstanding opera company. The move to Texas turned out to be a good one, but we knew that sometime in the future we would be returning to the West.

After attending several meetings of the board of regents, I realized that they were one of the main sources of problems with the Texas A&M system. At the time, they were largely visionless, political contributors or cronies of the governor (this hasn't changed much, I am told), and mostly comprised of Texas A&M graduates—Aggies! Most of them had little understanding of academics but thought they did, and their major interests seemed to be Aggie football and the Cadet Corps. (This is a once historically significant ROTC-like organization to which all students had to belong when A&M was an all male school, but now involves fewer than two thousand students with largely ceremonial responsibilities.) The issue of the need for academic tenure kept coming up and barely squeaked by on several votes. It is always a controversial issue with unenlightened governing boards.

The board's interest in the state of affairs of the other system universities bordered on the pathetic, except when it came to meddling in presidential searches. At the board meetings, it was embarrassing to watch the universities' presidents give their status reports to a largely disinterested board. A very dramatic moment occurred at one board meeting when the Prairie View A&M president, General Julius Becton, a very talented and highly decorated black Army officer, gave his retirement speech. He scorchingly lambasted the board for their racism, plantation-owner attitudes, and treatment of his fellow presidents and their universities.

This didn't seem to have much effect. Shortly thereafter I was given the responsibility of conducting a search for the new Prairie View A&M president, and an outstanding black senior engineer with administrative experience applied. The university faculty were very enthusiastic about his candidacy since they wanted to get away from military figures as presidents, and the search committee put him at the top of their list. But a week before the regents were to appoint the new president, they inserted the name of black general who was a Washington, D.C., bureaucrat with few accomplishments on the list of finalists, and then awarded him the presidency. The faculty were crestfallen, and even more so when he turned out to be a disaster, convinced that the university should be run like a boot camp.

My first boss was Chancellor William Mobley, former dean of the Texas A&M Business School, and an outstanding academic leader. With his support, and the collaborations I was establishing with the provosts of the system universities, I saw a bright future. We organized several excellent meetings to discuss academic programs and teaching evaluation, and Mobley and I had a very productive meeting with the south Texas Mexican American legislators. Everything was going well, but the regents were making Mobley's life miserable over some issues unknown to me. After six months on the job, he quit.

He was replaced by the president of one of the system universities, who was a sodbuster ex–school superintendent. He didn't believe in tenure and was an archetypical "good ol' boy"—a quality that seemed to be very attractive to some of the regents. One year later he called me into his office and asked, "Dr. Sánchez, do you consider yourself to be an academic?"

"Yes sir, I've always thought of myself as one," I replied.

"Well I don't need an academic in the system offices as a vice chancellor, so I'm giving you one month to find another job."

So in the spring of 1995, the administrative career of David Sánchez came to an end and his name could be insignificant once more.

CHAPTER FOURTEEN

ACADEME AND NEW MEXICO
THE FINAL VISIT

I returned to my first love, teaching and doing research in mathematics, with the help of Dr. Ray Bowen, president of Texas A&M, who had been one of my colleagues at the NSF. He helped arrange my appointment as full professor in the university's mathematics department. They were a little uneasy at first with an administrator in their ranks, but when I reverted back to my former ways as a teacher and researcher, they were at ease. I never set foot again in the system offices.

My teaching went well, and I recovered enough of my grey cells to write four research papers and a slim paperback on the teaching of differential equations. One of my highlights was teaching an honors course in calculus; ten students were enrolled, including three women. They were all very bright. I surprised them one day by bringing three slide rules to class and demonstrating their use. Then I let the students play with them. They were enthralled and spent the whole hour doing calculations; the added tactile element was clearly an attractor and much more challenging than pushing calculator keys.

One of my disappointments came teaching an introductory course in mathematics for forty-five prospective elementary and middle-school teachers and finding out through an informal poll that 40 percent didn't like mathematics. Many of them cited their high school geometry course as the reason for the start of their disaffection. I told them this dislike would probably rub off on their students and that maybe they should consider other careers. As I look at today's abysmal mathematics performance of our country's children, I think of that 40 percent.

Surprisingly, because of my thorough understanding of the NSF's proposal-review process, I became a valuable resource to the university and the system and assisted them in winning several multimillion dollar competitive grants in science and mathematics education, including one awarded to the mathematics department. The usual scenario was that a group of university faculty and administrators, the finalists for the award, would go to Washington to appear before a panel of experts to defend their proposal. I had the advantage of having observed the process many times and, after reading the proposal guidelines, would have a pretty good idea of what kinds of questions the panelists would ask. Especially important were the answers to questions of managing a large grant involving many administrative and research groups. Before the A&M group left for Washington, I would spend time rehearsing and grilling them, and we had positive results.

In 2000, Joan and I sold our house and moved into student apartments—two sixty-year-olds enveloped by rowdy Aggies on the weekend—and planned our retirement. We took a five-day drive around southern Colorado. We loved Pagosa Springs but it had no hospital facilities; Alamosa's winter temperatures matched Alaska's; Colorado Springs was far too conservative; we settled on returning to Albuquerque. Joan, who does all of our house purchasing, left to find a home, with my usual, minimal requirements: a small room for my books, a desk, and a bookcase that has been in my family since 1930, and a patio for summer barbecuing.

In 2001, I retired from Texas A&M and professional life, and we moved into a modest little home with an acre of sagebrush, rabbits, and roadrunners in Corrales, New Mexico. The combination of sagebrush and a little chamisa takes no care and perfectly complements my dislike of gardening. Corrales is a small village on the outskirts of Albuquerque with a kaleidoscopic mix of Hispanics, Anglos, farmers, winemakers, artists, equestrians, and retirees of all income levels, all zealously guarding their village from the encroachments of suburbia.

I volunteer in the very attractive Corrales Library once a week, served on their Friends board and on the board of the Corrales Cultural Arts Council, write, fish, play poker, duplicate bridge, and computer chess, and occasionally assist in workshops for local or regional mathematics teachers. I got my name in the newspaper for catching a big trout in the Chama River, attained the Life Master status in bridge, and finally, after many rejections, had one of my short stories published in the *Yale Anglers' Journal*. Having four grandchildren is also a very fulfilling experience, and I have good friends from my UNM undergraduate days with whom to share grandparenting tales and septuagenarian ailments.

As I look back on my career, I wonder whether the disquietude I have felt on and off for the last thirty-five years would have never appeared if I had decided to stay at UCLA and not taken up my advisory role to UMAS or better yet, had just decided to stay in Great Britain. I even wonder once in awhile how my life would have run its course if I had taken that job at Oregon State University right after graduate school. Clearly, there is a part of me that wants to belong to the simple academic life—a POP (plain ol' professor) as my wife says—where my last name is of no significance.

I definitely wonder whether the high-level, nonmathematical, administrative jobs and many national committee assignments I held would have been offered to me if my last name were, for instance, Anderson, Johnson, or Smith. It is bothersome; certainly Sánchez was the reason for the offers from Los Alamos and the Texas A&M system, and they were both awful experiences. But I did a good job and take personal pride that my intelligence and abilities probably exceeded whatever the position required. Most importantly, I guided or helped people. In 1995, I was very honored to receive the Bernard S. Rodey Award for leadership and success in higher education from the UNM Alumni Association.

I remember a party when I was on the UNM faculty. A group of us were entertaining a very talented Mexican American woman who was a social scientist. I was introduced to her and she very excitedly told me that I was an idol to her little sister, who was getting her PhD in microbiology. Back when I was at UCLA, I had attended a political party in East Los Angeles, got pretty bored, and spent part of the evening chatting with a young female junior high school student about careers in science. I had planted a seed and later found out that it had bloomed—there is no greater reward.

What about that accent mark? It's still there, perched above the "a." Sometimes persons accepting my check for a purchase, or reviewing a signed official document, look at my signature a little strangely and then look at me. Fair skinned, with a western American manner of speaking—the mismatch is bothersome. It can increase if I pronounce my last name in Spanish, with the "a" as in "father," as I frequently do.

Why do I persist in this? I believe that many of us of Mexican background, pure or mixed, fair or swarthy, bilingual or not, who have lived in this country for most of a lifetime, cherish a small reminder of our roots. It may be a picture of the Virgen de Guadalupe in our purse or wallet, or annual attendance at a Cinco de Mayo fiesta, or maybe a "Mi Casa Es Su Casa" plaque hanging in the kitchen. For me it is that accent mark.

I am proud of my Mexican heritage, happy to no longer be in the limelight, and content with being a slightly reclusive retired professor. I hope that my career opened paths for other talented individuals with names like Sánchez or Sanchez to lead this country's academic and scientific future.

APPENDIX

Committees and Service—Reminiscences of a Meeting Junkie

In the dossier of most people in my line of work, there will always be found a list of professional and university committees served as well as public-service participation. For important (real or believed to be) persons, the list will be long, often uninspired, and sometimes undecipherable. Do we need the list of the countless departmental committees? Is serving as treasurer of the neighborhood garden society relevant? What is the Society for Post-Hegelian Aesthetics? Some people seem to think that the number of assignments is a measure of their status.

This seems to apply as well to lists of publications, authored or coauthored, which for some professionals (e.g., chemists or life scientists) can run into the hundreds. They are often padded—the same article, with its title slightly altered, can appear in a journal, be part of a survey article, be presented at some panel discussion, then later appear in a book. I once read a bibliography in which a very senior educator included the title of his twelfth-grade term paper. Unless you are a real expert in the field, most of the titles will be meaningless. I have authored or coauthored over fifty mathematics research papers, books, and reviews, in English and Spanish; I leave these for the mathematically inclined readers to look up, if they wish.

Regarding my committee assignments and service, I decided to break the list down by the nature of the responsibilities and purpose and to provide some explanatory notes that describe their role in my career.

Governance

There are committees that serve as governing boards for professional societies; membership is usually by a contested election. The politics among peers can get tricky and sometimes passionate, and you have to watch out that they are not dominated by the senior members from prestigious institutions. Mathematicians regard themselves as pretty bright and therefore entitled to an opinion on any issue, so meetings can drag on and on. I represented applied mathematics and the Latino mathematics community, which was pretty small in those days.

Council of the American Mathematical Society, served 1979–1982

Board of Governors, Mathematical Association of America, served 1993–1995

Similarly elected or appointed committees govern non-mathematical professional societies; on these I was a representative mathematician and usually the only Latino. Undergraduate education, including better teaching preparation of faculty, was a major topic.

Board of Directors, American Association for Higher Education, served 1990–1994

The College Board, Academic Council, served 1997–2000

Advisory

Committees are appointed by professional societies and governmental agencies to provide advice in areas of interest. Some of these dealt solely with mathematics and mathematics education issues and were composed solely of my peers. After 1986, my background as a research mathematician, department chair, and provost provided some credibility, or suspicion, and I served on the following advisory groups:

**College Board Committee for the Advanced Placement
Examination in Calculus,** served 1982–1985

**American Mathematical Society Committee on Opportunities
in Mathematics for Disadvantaged Groups,** served 1970–1976

**Advisory Committee for the Mathematical Sciences Directorate,
National Science Foundation,** served 1987–1990

Other advisory appointments that had nothing to do with mathematics included:

Advisory Committee, Chicano Research Center, UCLA,
served 1974–1977

**Advisory Committee for the Education and Human
Resources Directorate, National Science Foundation,**
served 1993; chair 1998–19990

Selection

Committees to select candidates for fellowships from a pool of applicants were very exciting because one got to examine the dossiers of very talented young scholars, but in the early days there were no Latinos. Letters of recommendation were usually effusive, so one needed to know the school and the primary advisor. The committees were composed of top mathematicians, so agreement on selections went pretty smoothly, but loyalty to alma maters and one's own professors sometimes got in the way. I served on the following such committees:

**National Science Foundation Graduate Fellowship Selection
Committee—Mathematics,** served 1978–1980

Fulbright Fellowship Selection Panel in Mathematics,
served 1979–1981, 1984–1986

**National Science Foundation Postdoctoral Fellowship
Selection Committee—Mathematics,** served 1978–1980

Service

Like any responsible faculty member, I served on a number of university committees dealing with issues like curriculum, academic planning, promotion, and searches for new faculty or administrators. This experience helped very much when I moved into academic administration, but the committee work I enjoyed the most had nothing to do with the university or my last name but helped enrich the community, such as the following:

Board of Directors, Lehigh Valley Chamber Orchestra,
served 1990–1992

Advisory Board, National Museum of American Art, served 1994

Corrales Cultural Arts Council, served 2002–2005

Friends of the Corrales Library, served 2008–2009

Shepherd of the Valley Presbyterian Church,
Mission Committee, served 2008–2010

Board, Martinez House of Neighborly Services, 2008–2010